REV. ROBERT C. COOK

When The Sun Comes Up in the West

A Missionary's New Song of Justice and Peace

Douglas Maben, Editor

WestBow
PRESS

Copyright © 2011 Rev. Robert C. Cook

All rights reserved. No part of this book may be used or reproduced by any means, graphic, electronic, or mechanical, including photocopying, recording, taping or by any information storage retrieval system without the written permission of the publisher except in the case of brief quotations embodied in critical articles and reviews.

New Revised Standard Version Bible, copyright 1989, Division of Christian Education of the National Council of the Churches of Christ in the United States of America. Used by permission. All rights reserved.

WestBow Press books may be ordered through booksellers or by contacting:

WestBow Press
A Division of Thomas Nelson
1663 Liberty Drive
Bloomington, IN 47403
www.westbowpress.com
1-(866) 928-1240

Because of the dynamic nature of the Internet, any web addresses or links contained in this book may have changed since publication and may no longer be valid. The views expressed in this work are solely those of the author and do not necessarily reflect the views of the publisher, and the publisher hereby disclaims any responsibility for them.

Any people depicted in stock imagery provided by Thinkstock are models, and such images are being used for illustrative purposes only.

Certain stock imagery © Thinkstock.

ISBN: 978-1-4497-3138-0 (sc)
ISBN: 978-1-4497-3139-7 (hc)
ISBN: 978-1-4497-3137-3 (e)

Library of Congress Control Number: 2011961164

Printed in the United States of America

WestBow Press rev. date: 12/27/2011

This book is dedicated to my grandchildren, those who are among us today, and those who are yet to be, who are the greatest loves of my life.

"Our father has been a source of inspiration since we were young children. We have been blessed by having such a stellar example in life. He preaches doing the right thing, treating others with respect, and helping anyone in need, and he then goes above and beyond his words. This makes being his sons and raising his grandchildren an honor. We have uttered the following words many times over the years: 'When I grow up, I hope to be half the man my father is.' This still holds true in our hearts."

—Steven and Jason Cook, Bob's Sons

Thoughts

"Bob's deep faith and political awareness makes reading *When the Sun Comes Up in the West* a necessity for anyone wanting to understand the past decade of El Salvador's history."

—Rev. Don Elly, Pastor

"Bob Cook's name is synonymous with social justice—with faith in action. He has walked the walk in Iowa, and did so in El Salvador. The reader will be forever changed."

—Charlotte B. Nelson, former Executive Director, Iowa Commission on the Status of Women

"Robert Cook is a man driven by a heart that desires nothing more than to be employed in the work of the Kingdom of God."

—Rev. Duane "Doc" Skidmore

Contents

Foreword		ix
Preface		xiii
Introduction		xxi
Chapter 1	The Sun Rose In The West	1
Chapter 2	Sixteen Days of Heartbreak	18
Chapter 3	A Return Visit	36
Chapter 4	No One Is an Island	49
Chapter 5	Out Of The Shadows	57
Chapter 6	Rooting the Mustard Seed	68
Chapter 7	Blood Soaked Soil	78
Chapter 8	Dark Night of My Soul	87
Chapter 9	Woman in the Blue Dress	104
Chapter 10	Get Out of Jail Free Card	112
Chapter 11	Claudia Nadina's Miracle	118
Chapter 12	The Beginning of Our Sister Parish Mission	128
Chapter 13	The Seed Grows First Projects and Growth in Mission	131
Chapter 14	The Celebrations and Tears of Micro-business	152
Chapter 15	My Family Grows (Unofficially)	161
Chapter 16	Postscript Undocumented Immigrants	182
Acknowledgements		189
Editor's Note		193

Foreword

Before Bob Cook decided to go to El Salvador to live, he told me that his awareness of a sense of call to do so dated back to a time when he heard me speak on Latin America, some years before. Though I didn't remember, from the many times and places when or where it might have been, I felt a nudge of responsibility for what he might encounter on his venture. Having experienced the beginning of the "Dirty Little War" in Argentina, with its military coup and dictatorship, which resulted in the disappearance, torture and murder of thousands of Argentine citizens; I still remember vividly, that more frightening still were the times I spent in El Salvador in 1987 and 1994. Given the reality there, one never knew whether the next corner turned might be one's last! So, whatever my words sparked in the readiness of Bob's mind to hear, opening it to that decision in his life's direction, the least I could answer to his request to write a forward for his book was, "Yes." Now, having read the full manuscript in one sitting, I can truly say that it is an amazing and compelling story!

Those of us who were present at his retirement/going away party probably harbored some skepticism about his venture's advisability. Without knowing Spanish, having been in a Latin American culture only for temporary visits, and without the training and the support of a mainline denominational mission board (he would likely be considered too old to begin, and no Presbyterian Churches even existing in that country to receive him), the project looked a little like Don Quixote charging out to tilt at windmills. Given the well-known dangers of El Salvador, where a gringo stands out as a target, for deeply felt resentment toward the Yankee support of the oppressive ruling oligarchy, Bob's choice looked a little suicidal. His attitude was and is too humble to give him the pretension of being a Lone Ranger savior for the poor and oppressed of El Salvador and, even though his skin color marked him, he lacked the visible means of structured support most North American's would take with them, and most certainly he was not mounted on a white horse. To the credit of the Des Moines Presbytery, however, he did go with their blessing and their willingness to receive and disperse funds given on behalf of his work.

However, to think that Bob went without preparation would be a mistake. Those who had known him over the years knew of his work at Cross Ministries with poor and disenfranchised persons in Des Moines. Many throughout the State had known, and been supportive of, his ministry at Hansen House, which he brought to fruition to address the needs of ex-offenders attempting to reenter life on the outside. His repeated trips with organizations to El Salvador, and his return to interpret the reality there with persons in churches here, while also serving very effectively in interim pastorates, attested to his patient skill, and faithful commitment.

All of these non-profit ministries, through which he and others sought to meet the needs of the most disadvantaged among us, cause one to go beyond mere charitable response, to question the causes, which give rise to the need in the first place. More often than not, whatever personal responsibility the one who receives may bear, the roots are embedded in systemic injustice in which we are all involved in one way or another. The magnitude of this involvement is multiplied many fold when it comes to our nation's historic involvement with Latin America in general, and Bob, in beginning this trek, was no stranger to that history.

Nevertheless, time and again, he is confronted by his own naïveté and the sense that he too is an "ugly American," in spite of himself. What is meant by this phrase, "ugly American," is that part of the culture shock of living and working with the poor and oppressed of "Third World" countries, is the recurring awareness that we, as the privileged of the "First World" USA, assume a monolithic mindset. We are usually unaware of it, until those who have disproportionally born the burden of our privilege confront us. We just automatically assume that our worldview is reality, and that we have the answers to the dilemmas, which the disadvantaged need to learn if they will only listen.

Furthermore, we have the technology and ingenuity to make things happen and that, with patience, they can be where we are with our help. Our foreign aid to poor, "underdeveloped" countries, which we presume has been far above any benefit we might have received in return, should have more than balanced the scales of justice and fairness.

In no way was Bob that unaware of the unfairness of "free trade" and the institutions that perpetuate and deepen the unfairness. Nor was he unaware of the "chain mailed fist" of enforcement through our overseas military bases and installations, such as our Fourth Fleet, previously located in the Panama Canal Zone, along with the School of the Americas. He was well aware that Latin American military high command and officer core have long been trained in assassination and "enhanced interrogation," more commonly known as torture which is still being carried out at Ft. Benning, Georgia and elsewhere under another name. Their responsibility for the torture and death of teachers, labor leaders, community activists, priests, nuns, and Archbishop Romero of El Salvador itself, are well known worldwide, but not considered credible by the mindset, which still prevails in our own country.

That however is not what Bob meant when he speaks of his own naïveté, and tendency to Ugly American moments. His ability to bring others along in acknowledging our national naïveté and historical amnesia, regarding our blind spots of selective ignorance and the suffering they have caused, is testified to by his success in interpreting in these pages what he learned first hand in Latin America. His honesty and humility enables him to see himself as part of the problem, and to speak of systemic injustice as a "we," "ours," and "us" problem from which we have great difficulty escaping. It is our almost automatic, monolithic mindset that causes us to continue to speak before listening to, and experiencing, what the dispossessed have lived; and to think we have the answers if they will only listen to us and do as we say.

Bob would say that, by the grace of God, his very weaknesses turned out to be the source of his greatest strength. Not knowing neither the language nor the culture, he could only sit under the shade of a tree day after day, looking, listening and feeling what was going on around him, in a remote, rural village, in guerrilla occupied territory. His total dependence on the poor inhabitants of that cantón to sustain, protect, and ultimately save his life, enabled him to absorb something of the helplessness and hopelessness of their own circumstances. In those days of mute interaction and deepening introspection, a growing sense of mutual trust finally enabled him to discover, in his own buried unconscious self, a hurt at the heart of his own sensitivity. He had found his own freedom in sensing and siding with them in their helplessness and hurt, until the mutual sharing of hurt would give rise to hope for all! Even in the absorbing of more pain and suffering together in community there is the will to survive and overcome the entrenched powers of greed and arrogance.

Not surprisingly, all the way through the recounting of these anecdotal experiences the reader is encouraged to understand them in the context of ancient Jewish and Christian texts from the Bible, which these monotheistic faiths, along with Islam, share in common. And interspersed throughout are passages that echo, in our time and place, the same call to faith in practice now.

In addition we are urged to read between the lines that link the stories together, the facts and their ultimate historical meaning of which Bob shares with us through his own interpretation. If WikiLeaks has published to the world the hidden conversations and plans of the powerful for world domination, then these stories and many others like them, picture the spirit of the powerless who indeed have no choice but to resist that domination. And united they cannot ultimately be defeated, for the Realm of God, and the common good, will only be realized when the last, least and lost are put first, and the first, the finest, and the founded are put last!

Read at your own risk, for it may change forever your own way of life!

Then pass it on!

Gil Dawes
July, 2011

Gil Dawes is an activist pastor and long-time, valued associate of Bob Cook. For his entire career he has centered his ministry on the fight for justice, whether it be on behalf of the poor, minorities, workers or others subjugated by United States imperialism. Now retired, he, along with his wife Inez, continue to focus their faith around issues of justice, peace and civil rights.

Preface

El Salvador: The Country and Its People

Nestled between Guatemala and Honduras, El Salvador, which in Spanish translates "The Savior", is the tiniest of all the Central American counties. Anyone who is able to move his or her attention beyond the heartbreak of poverty that racks the country will be taken by the beauty of a mountainous terrain that is covered with a lush green during the six-month rainy season from May to November. That beautiful green is turned to a dust laden brownish-green landscape during the dry season of the other six months of the year. Through the center of the country runs a mountain range and Central Plateau consisting of a series of volcanoes. It is a country no larger than one-sixth the size of the state of Iowa, so it is no wonder that within an hour of any location in El Salvador, one can be relaxing on one of the many beautiful beaches along the Pacific coast. Within the mountainous terrain there are eight active volcanoes with an eruption of one, the Santa Ana Volcano, as recently as 2006, causing two deaths and hundreds of homeless from the villages. The more devastating of natural disasters are earthquakes. There are many tiny tremors that go seemingly unnoticed during each week. The last destructive earthquake took place in 2001, killing over one thousand people and leaving many thousands homeless.

The many dirt floor huts that serve as homes for the poor are evidence the high level of poverty in El Salvador. It is not uncommon for them to be constructed of scavenged materials, such as sheet metal, cardboard, or plywood, though many are built of cement block or adobe. Innumerable families exist with no electricity or potable water. Every morning, people awaken to the job of walking for hours to carry the water necessary for life to their homes, a task that generally falls upon the women of the community. Hundreds of shacks dot the mountainsides and entire communities of shacks, known as cantónes[1], are common in the surrounding areas of pueblos throughout the country.

Oppression and War

In 1984, the tiny Central American country of El Salvador became a "puppet democracy" of the United States. For decades, prior to that year, El Salvador had been a "puppet dictatorship," with the United States propping up the oppressive regimes that always treated the poor among them with distain and oppression. For centuries, fourteen extended families owned and controlled the land and resources of the country, which, in turn, controlled an oligarchy consisting of government, military, and church rule. Death squads became the feared instruments of control in the mid-twentieth century. United States foreign policy supported the violent practices of the government by providing training for death squads at School of the Americas, originally located in Panama, then later moved to Fort Benning, Georgia. The school has become quite controversial in recent years, but continues to be defended by the State Department as a necessary support to budding democracies like El Salvador, casting them under the guise of being defenders of such democracies. Death squads would strike anyone who publicly raised a voice for basic human rights, education, health care, or employment. By limiting these human dignities, the poor continued to be uneducated and lacked any avenue by which to better their lives. Thus, they were always abundant and readily available as cheap labor to the small, wealthy, and politically powerful class of El Salvador. To this day, the poor are oppressed by coffee and

---

1   Cantónes are dirt floor home communities that in Iowa would be the equivalent of towns that surround a metropolitan area. Berlin in this case is the "city" and the cantons the towns in a ten by ten square kilometer area. Access to potable water is limited, and most of the cantons do not have electricity. The only access to medical care is health promoters who have little to no medicines to prescribe, nor medical equipment for examinations. Nor are there commercial areas where groceries and other home needs can be purchased. What goods and services are available to the Salvadoran poor are found in the municipality of Berlin.

sugar cane plantation owners, who use their guaranteed cheap labor to maximize their own profits. The country's inadequate three dollars per day legislated minimum wage does not apply to the agricultural sector, which means those who labor in coffee and sugar cane harvests are lucky to receive two dollars per day.

The extreme conditions of poverty, the injustices born on a daily basis, and the daily death squad hits, especially in the rural areas, made a civil war inevitable. Organizing against the human rights violations by the government began to take shape after the bishops at the Council of Medéllin in 1968 declared God's "preferential treatment of the poor," which gave rise to the grassroots movement that came to be identified as Liberation Theology. The bishops, in their declaration of faith, stated that the poor have a right to have basic human needs provided through a just and compassionate order. The oligarchy of church/government/military rejected that premise and even went as far as to say poverty was God's will and their suffering in poverty in mortal life would be rewarded in the afterlife in heaven. Since their poverty was God's will, to protest and try to change their poverty conditions would be considered a protest against God. The new liberation theology focus established at the council brought a new awareness to the poor and that God, in fact, calls for justice and the establishing of a basic set of values that recognized the needs of the poor as human beings in this life.

As the poor became more aware, they began to organize to resist the long-established denial of their essential rights in life. In response, the Salvadoran government increased its oppression of the poor by initiating a campaign of terror against the poor, with expanded use of the U.S.-trained death squads to terrorize the poor and those who spoke up on behalf of the poor. Yet, it did not deter the campaign led by the poor and their sympathizers to organize resistance to government oppression. By the early 1970s, five political opponent groups existed throughout the country to oppose the sanctioned violence. By the late 1970s, those five groups had united as the FMLN (Farabundo Marti National Liberation Front), later to become known throughout the world as the revolutionary movement that launched a twelve-year civil war in El Salvador. It was Farabundo Marti who in 1932 had planted the seeds of resistance in the ongoing struggle of the poor. He was the leader of an uprising known as the Coffee Rebellion of 1932 that resulted in the massacre of as many as thirty thousand indigenous El Salvadorans, who refused to pick coffee at the very low wages offered. Thus Marti was and is a folk hero in the long and historic struggle for Salvadoran human rights.

With the martyrdom of Monsignor Oscar Romero on March 24, 1980, the beginning of El Salvador's civil war was indelibly stamped on its history. With American public opinion beginning to turn against involvement in El Salvador, United States foreign policy, in keeping with its practice of propping up Third World oppressive and petty dictatorships, joined forces with the oligarchy's political party ARENA, then in power. In their fight to rid the country of the rebels, their propaganda labeled them as no more than "drug-running delinquents," under the disguise of a democratic freedom movement who called themselves FMLN. To insure victory, the United States sent one to two million dollars per day to pay for El Salvador's government-sanctioned war against the poor.

With nothing to lose and essential human rights as the prize, the FMLN gained in numbers and military strength. All the while, the Salvadoran government persisted in describing the battles taking place in the rural areas as no more than arresting "drug running delinquents;" and it was just a matter of time until the FMLN would be eliminated. In November, 1989, the FMLN brought the war into the capital city of San Salvador, and the strength and military might of the revolutionaries was exposed to the world. That same month, the murders of six Jesuit professors at the University of Central America, along with their housekeeper and her daughter, attributed to government- sanctioned death squad activity, which, in turn, brought about an international outcry for the Salvadoran government to cease its atrocities of torture and death. That left the U.S. no option but to insist with the ruling government (which in 1984 became a democracy) to enter into peace negotiations with the FMLN.

In 1992, peace accords were signed between the Salvadoran government and the FMLN. Those accords recognized the FMLN as an official political party. Also, there was land reform, which provided an avenue for the poor to own land. But the reality of poverty remained a constant, and some say it is worse today than it was at the beginning of the war in

1980. Few significant social changes seem to have taken hold thus far in this impoverished nation. But it is significant that eighteen years after the signing of the peace accords, the FMLN is the ruling party in the legislative assembly and an FMLN presidential candidate was elected to power in 2008. Still, even with a political party that is sympathetic to the poor being in power, the reality of the world's economic conditions makes challenging poverty's hold extremely difficult. On a positive note, the government in 2010 initiated a program to provide uniforms, notebooks, and other basic education needs to parents whose children attend national schools.

An interesting factor in economic difficulties of the poor is tied directly to the land reform provision in the peace accords. Historically, there were fourteen families who owned or controlled land of El Salvador. With control of land now less certain, six of the fourteen families controlling most of the country's wealth have moved their economic interests from land to other sectors of the economy. Their investments became goods and services, including pharmaceuticals, fertilizer, and communications. With that controlling advantage, they have now succeeded in privatizing those interests, which allows them to drive their prices and profits higher, thus making the cost of living even more out of reach for the poor. With the cost of living rapidly increasing month to month, more and more families were left with the decision of who would be the one they send to make their way north to the U.S. to find work, and to send money home to El Salvador for survival.

Poverty and Immigration

The average cost of living for a middle class family of four in El Salvador is $12,000 annually. Sixty percent of the population is poor, and their meager income barely covers the cost of the canasta (basic foods of beans, corn, and rice). That alone is the motivating factor that causes an increasing number of people to find their way to the United States, in a desperate search for economic survival. It is estimated that currently two and a half million Salvadorans have made the dangerous and expensive trip to the United States to find work since the end of hostilities in the country. The money they send home to family and friends, referred to by the Salvadoran government and economic community as *remenses*, amounted to over 3.4 billion dollars in 2007 alone. It is becoming an increasingly important line item in the Salvadoran economy.

The controversy of the illegal status of immigrants has overshadowed the reality of poverty and human need that has driven men and women to make the dangerous trip. Families sell what they have and borrow at a high rate of interest from those with resources to pay a coyote (person who becomes the guide for the dangerous trip) up to seven thousand dollars for safe passage. For many families, this is decided after an attempt to get a visa from the U.S. Embassy in San Salvador. The cost for a visa is, at present, one hundred and fifteen dollars, plus fifteen more for one or more required phone cards, purchased at Banco Cuscatlán, which then arrange for the appointment with the U.S. Embassy for the visa interview, with computers connected to the appointment office at the embassy. Given that ninety-seven percent of the three hundred applicants daily are denied a Visa, and the cost to apply is not returned in cases of denial, it is no wonder many don't even make the attempt to apply.

I personally have witnessed the fracturing of families caused by this need to emigrate. On the day of departure for the arduous journey, the family gathers for a last meal together. The tears of mothers and other adult women of the extended family flow as they prepare to give one of their own up to the economic beast of survival. Fathers display little emotion, but pain and fear fill their eyes, and their lips quiver with the knowledge they will not see their son or daughter possibly for years, perhaps never again. Brothers and sisters assure that they will follow to be with them when money and time permit. The immorality of this tragedy should not focus on the fact that they are illegal immigrants breaking the U.S. laws of immigration, but rather the corruption of a political and economic system, largely neglected by the U.S., following a huge investment in a destructive war that caused the tragedy in the beginning. Of course, the two-faced nature of U.S. industry and commerce, on one hand encouraging the stream of undocumented workers to risk their lives, so that cheap labor is still available in the United States, while at the same time bemoaning the cost to many of these companies, and to the social fabric of the U.S., because of the additional demands placed on hospitals, schools, and other services paid for with U.S. tax dollars. It is simply a new form of slavery that marches on, south to north.

I would argue that it is not the emigrants who are at fault, but that illegal emigration is a deliberate creation of misguided government policies and private investments driven by the greed that demands cheaper and cheaper labor. The addendum on Undocumented Immigrants provides a brief explanation of those policies and how they became the driving force for the poor to seek employment in the U.S., thus becoming refugees and strangers living in a strange land.

The Creation of the Gang Culture

Violence and delinquency are continuing and growing concerns for the people of El Salvador. Gangs have become a form of "street Mafia" of El Salvador. Their threat is significant and was cause for the National Police Force to institute what was known as *Mano Duro* or "hard hand" in 2004. The police swept the areas where gangs are known to exist and arrested anyone who had a tattoo, which is an identification mark of gang membership. It is not uncommon to see young men detained on the street by police, being searched and harassed without cause or warrant. The effect of this Gestapo-style of treatment has driven a wedge of resentment deeply between street people and the police.

Gangs are an outgrowth of the civil war. Many families fled the country, making their way to large cities in the United States, cities like Los Angeles, Dallas, Miami, and Washington D.C. There the teenagers joined existing U.S. Salvadoran gangs. Commonly, that gang is referred to as MS (Mara Salvatrucha) or M13. When the war was over and they returned to their native land or were deported by U.S. immigration authorities, the knowledge and membership of gangs went with the young men and women who returned to El Salvador. There, gangs began to recruit members from the poverty- stricken youth who had little opportunity to find work or receive an education. The gang became their "family," and the fierce rule for loyalty among members made them a growing force of delinquency within the Salvadoran society. There are levels of gangs, with distinct names according to their function. Some younger or new recruits are the street delinquents that rob unsuspecting victims in crowds and at stoplights. Once they make a name for themselves in the gang, they move up into the more powerful sector of gang life that controls areas of the city, often charging "rent" for buses to pass or for businesses to exist. Banks, super markets, and other major business interests employ armed guards to protect them from robbery. Private security is now one of the largest sources of employment in El Salvador. Gangs have become powerful with networking throughout Central America and to the cities of the United States. In 2006, the FBI set up an office in San Salvador to assist in the battle of growing delinquency that is taking on the power of a well-organized group, thus the term "street Mafia."

God's Preference for the Poor: A Call for Justice

In the following chapters, I have written of the experiences and thoughts of my life in El Salvador. As I began to live that call of God to know Salvadoran poverty and to ultimately live my life with them, I knew little of what I have written here about El Salvador. I had a steep learning curve about the country and the poverty, the likes of which I had never before seen or experienced. At first, it broke my heart, and then transformed my sense of ministry and the depth of my faith to empower me to live out the message of love and justice taught by Jesus. These memoirs represent more than two decades since my first trip to El Salvador in November, 1990.

Paul writes in Corinthians, *"There are many gifts but it is the same Spirit that gives them"* (1 Cor. 12.4), which points out that not all people are called in the same way. My decision to follow my heart to live with the poor of El Salvador in no way suggests such a move is right for all people of faith. But I challenge anyone who, either by fate or conscious decision, experiences extreme poverty to be unaffected by it and be able to ignore the call for preferential treatment of the poor. To experience that kind of poverty will necessarily result in one's own examination of lifestyle and how one can be moved to live out the prophet Micah's call: *"What does the Lord require of you, but that you do justice, to love kindness, and to walk humbly with your God."* To do otherwise is to deny God who lives within us.

Introduction

"I am neither a prophet, nor the son of a prophet,.." I am but a common man,.. and the Lord said to me, go speak to my people."
Amos 7.14-15

I am a retired missionary to El Salvador for Des Moines Presbytery. I never felt a desire to live in a foreign country, nor was I enamored with the vision of a missionary vocation. Nevertheless, from 1990 to 1999, by fate, design and spiritual movement I was immersed in a quest to know the political and social dynamics of Third World poverty; which became the force of change that made El Salvador the focus of my new faith journey.

The genesis of my decision to move to Berlin, El Salvador, to work with the Parish Team of the Parish of St. Joseph began in November of 1990. That was the year I visited the Cantón El Tablón, a community of dirt-floor homes, which is one of the seventeen cantónes on the mountainside in the municipality of Berlin. El Tablón had been chosen by Des Moines Presbytery to receive 50% of its 1990 Rural Harvest Offering, an offering designed to impact hunger by providing developmental resources for selected projects in developing countries. As Hunger Action Enabler for the Presbytery part of the responsibilities was to write promotional materials for the offering. The visit to El Tablón grew out of my certainty that, by seeing first-hand the poverty of a developing nation, I could do a better job of promoting the Hunger Offering in the ensuing years. El Tablón came to be the catalyst of a new spiritual direction in my life and ministry. My visit to that cantónes changed me forever.

When I made that trip in 1990, El Salvador was in the tenth year of the civil war. My visit to El Tablón taught me of the fear that can imprison the souls of the innocent, especially women and children, caught in the midst of the combat of war. The sixteen days I lived with the residents of El Tablón taught me that poverty has a repugnant odor, its sounds are disconcerting and the sight of it instills mental anguish that brings silent sobs in the night. Environmentally, it is a scene that melds into an array of discontent and disorder. It erodes the foundation of the soul, and eventually evolves into a surrealistic aberration of reality and life.

I sat many hours under a large tree in front of the home where I slept. The tree is my personal monument that marks the place where a truth gradually seeped into my soul bringing about an unfathomable dismay, and an affront to what has been conveyed to people through the political propaganda of the United States to excuse funding for El Salvador's war against the poor, the convenient lie told over and over again that Communist revolutionaries were fighting for control of the El Salvadoran government and its people. In this way the revolutionaries could recreate El Salvador as a staging area for the Communist march through Mexico to invade the U.S. Over and over again I witnessed consequences of extreme poverty in the lives of the people of El Tablón. What I saw belied any truth to the invasion scenario, and more logically the revolution was a grass roots movement to liberate the poor from oppressive poverty.

From the shade of my tree, I witnessed two women tie a gaping machete wound shut with a strip of cloth from a t-shirt, a little girl whimper from pain of a jaw swollen caused by an abscessed tooth, a mother worry for the life of a baby with uncontrollable diarrhea; a child with a stomach distended from malnutrition and no medical care for anyone, anywhere. Sadness or fear, or maybe both replaced the sparkle in the eye of many children. A tortilla for lunch was common, there were no sweets for children, let alone a balanced diet to quell the ever-present pang of hunger and provide for a child's proper growth and development. There was not a day that any child went off to school because the war had made it too dangerous for any travel to the school that went only to the sixth grade; and besides the building had been fallen into disuse and lack of repair due to the war economy eating away and human resources. These were only some of the daily worries of a people of whom Jesus said, "Blessed are the poor." At that point, in time the primary motivation of their lives was survival. Education would have to come later.

Bob in the shade of his tree

For certain, there was more I witnessed but, by the fourth day. I had learned more about third world poverty than I had bargained for and I simply wanted to go home. I yearned to go home. I was aching to go home. I counted the days when I could walk away from it all and never have to look back. I checked the calendar...twelve days, and my heart filled with despair.

If the house where I slept still stood it would be the monument rather than the tree. It was in that house that I experienced the dynamics of Jesus' words: *"You shall know the truth, and the truth will set you free."* Truth I learned one night, sitting and conversing with five women that set me free from a brutal violence that had cowered in protective denial within me for five decades. The truth of that remembered brutality united me with Salvadoran poor on a seemingly common ground that I needed in order to complete my education about third world poverty. It would be the penultimate point that would ensure that I would never be able to walk away from what I had learned in those few days and not look back. The truth, my own truth that I rediscovered, and the power of that moment with those women, is written of later in the book. It would take many months for it to be fully known, but it began to emerge in my memory briefly that night in El Tablón. And it was indeed the truth of brutalization that bridged time and space to define a mutual affirmation of life between me and the poor of El Salvador. I considered long and hard as to whether I should include this part of my story in these writings. My best friends, Doug Maben and Frank Cordaro convinced me this knowledge of brutalizing violence was key to the telling of my story. It took more than a year of counseling for me to heal those memories.

Each year, until 1999, I visited El Salvador. Sometimes I led delegations in order to educate them of the reality of the poverty with which Salvadorans lived. Sometimes I went alone. Always, always, I felt the pull to act, to *"do something,"* but resources were limited for making much of an impact on the incredible privation of that land and its people. I took it one year at a time. From my perspective in the early 1990s, I could not imagine what the years ahead would bring. I only knew that the poverty I encountered each time I returned to El Salvador brought more disquiet to my soul and a greater sense of unity with the poor of El Salvador.

The moment of decision came one evening in the winter of 1999. Cold winds whipped at my face and the darkness of the season set the stage for what began to illumine my mind. I had been locked out of my home and circumstances were that only by breaking a window could I access the comfort of warmth inside. I sensed conflict stir in my soul. My discomfort in the cold was a moment in time. But poverty is a barrier to all comforts all the time. The refrain, "God hears the cry of the poor" became a reoccurring echo in the silence of the night and from it came the conscious recognition of what had been until then an unspoken tug in my heart. I was being called to live with the poor in El Salvador.

I began a process of putting my life in such an order as would allow me to move to the mountainside in eastern El Salvador, to that place called Berlin. It took me two years to complete that task. The message I received that night was to leave behind my preconceptions of what my life is, or should be, and allow the Spirit to recreate my way of life. So, without the knowledge of how, or from where the resources would come, I chose to accept the call to a life journey that only faith can initiate. It was faith alone that allowed me to believe that the resources would come, and that God's grace would prevail in my plans to move away from the area I had called home for fifty-eight years. Words written by the theologian and martyr Dietrich Bonhoeffer, come to mind: *"What does it mean to believe, I mean, in-so-far as we might be willing to give our life for it?"*[2]

In the beginning, ignorance reigned regarding my knowledge of Salvadoran life. And it would have been presumptuous of me to say I had an exact plan for implementing a new life in El Salvador, let alone to build a mission of social development that continues to this day under the leadership of a board known as Compañeros. Yes, I had the assurance of my Salvadoran friends, who made up the Parish Team, and with whom I lived and worked for the basics of food and shelter. They also assured me I would, in time, learn how to speak the language and I would learn the culture and customs of the land. So I moved forward with all the hope I possessed that this new life would come together. For over two years I made preparations for the life-changing move. As the time grew closer I began to sense a deep sadness. At times I questioned my sanity in making such a drastic change so late in life. Especially in the dark of night, and private moments of reflection, my anticipation of the adventure ahead was trumped by sadness as I pondered what it would be like to be so far from my sons, Steven and Jason, and my many friends in the church and community, and a root of my life that was fifty-eight years deep. At times it was a lonely trek I had claimed for my future. But my sons and many friends encouraged and supported me, and their frequent statements of pride instilled a sense of awe and wonder at what lay before me. So I moved on, and I can say that I never looked back, except there was a moment during my Des Moines to Atlanta flight, somewhere over Georgia, when the utter weight of what I had chosen struck me. For that moment, high in the air, between the world I had known and the world I would come to know, I felt a bit lost; unable to return to my former life and not quite prepared to embrace an unknown future. But the moment passed. I was never again to be haunted by such thoughts.

---

2   Dietrich Bonhoeffer, Letters and Papers from Prison.

This is the story of my journey, based on sixteen years of reflections that bring into focus my Salvadoran life and experiences. It begins with my first visit to El Salvador in 1990. In what I write, I hope to portray a candid reflection of my walk, a reflection of faith experiences, devastating moments, fears, surges of hope and life-changing challenges with Jesus Christ as my guide.

Chapter 1

The Sun Rose In The West

"How shall we sing the Lord's song in a strange land?"
Ps. 137.4

It was my first trip outside the United States. It would be an understatement to say I was nervous. As the plane taxied to its designated place for passengers to deplane, I could see the large sign that welcomed travelers to El Salvador. My discomfort turned to unnerving apprehension when I saw a camouflaged tank rolling up to the plane. Next came a dozen or so soldiers with M-16 rifles to establish a security perimeter against an unseen enemy. It all set the scene for a reality far exceeding whatever education and experience my forty-seven years had offered me. It was not the sort of thing one usually saw when disembarking in Des Moines, Iowa. The comfort of my white, male, middle-class American life had collided with violent truth. It would repeat itself in many pensive moments in the twenty-nine day trip that lay ahead. Today, as I write these thoughts from the many Salvadoran experiences I have had over the past two decades, I realize that it was those twenty-nine days that changed my life--and my mission in life--forever.

Every seat on the 727 passenger plane was occupied. Most were gringos who had come to participate in the first anniversary of the murder of six Jesuit priests and two women at the University of Central America. The silence among my fellow travelers suggested that the military greeting we had all just experienced was beyond almost everyone's frame of reference for deplaning. The cabin was filled with an isolating, deafening silence. The significance of the days ahead began to take on a different meaning in my mind. What I had imagined to be an adventure had been transformed into a journey of vague insecurity.

We deplaned, and I followed in line with other passengers to immigration. The line of foreigners snaked its way through a dingy and poorly lit airport, down a non-functioning escalator to a large open area filled with what I estimated to be two hundred visitors to El Salvador. It seemed an eternity for it to become my turn with the immigration official behind darkened windows and thick walls. It was another eternity for him to review the thirty-day visa I had stamped in my passport from the Chicago Salvadoran Embassy. Even though I could not see the person's face behind the smoked glass, I sensed I was not welcome. None of us was welcome. At that moment, I did not much care if he denied my visa and sent me home, thus putting an end to the shades of nightmarish moments that were clouding my mind.

The pound of his official stamp on my passport broke the silence and signaled that finally the official behind the sea of blackness had permitted me to travel in his country. I was such a novice at traveling in foreign countries; I assumed I had thirty days, as that is what the Salvadoran Embassy in Chicago had stamped in my passport some weeks earlier. So I did not even look at the number until eleven days later. I had been given twelve days on my visa. Twelve days to be in the country legally. By not having a valid Salvadoran visa, I actually lived illegally in El Salvador for eighteen days of my trip.

The airport was stuffy and dirty. Today it has been converted into a clean and modern facility, which some say is the best airport in Central America. My first stop beyond immigration was the bathroom. The odor reminded me of the outhouses of my youth in rural Iowa. Baskets in each stall overflowed with used toilet paper. This was done in order to avoid having the paper clog up the pipes when flushed down the stool. Sanitation in the Third World is an educational process, and El Salvador is still learning about it even today. It was an easy decision to postpone my bathroom needs, and I moved on to the luggage carousel to retrieve my two suitcases. The line of bags inched forward, each suitcase's contents examined for contraband, weapons, drugs, or whatever the representatives of the Salvadoran government decided to arbitrarily decline. I felt some apprehension, because one of my suitcases was filled with medicines and educational supplies for the Cantón El Tablón at Berlin, reason enough to be detained for interrogation by airport security.

My turn for inspection came. The man doing the baggage inspection was armed and numerous soldiers were standing about, nearby, armed with M-16 rifles. To say it was an unfriendly welcome would be to grossly understate the moment. He waved for me to stand back as he unzipped the first suitcase containing the medicines. He pawed through the many bottles, and without exchanging words; I knew he wanted the bottle of aspirin he held in his palm. I nodded my approval and indicated that he could take another if he wished. I would have given him half the contents of the suitcase at that point just to get beyond the intense, unfamiliar clamor of the immigration process. It seemed like very cheap fare for my passage into the world of El Salvador. I was waved on through.

Gigi Grunke, a staff person for the SHARE Foundation, had made the arrangements for my trip. Tony, the man she had arranged to transport me to San Salvador, was waiting outside the airport with a sign that read *"Robert Cuk."* It was close enough, and I was very happy to be greeted by a friendly face, and especially relieved to discover that his face spoke English. I deeply appreciated the moment of lucidity. There would be few of them in the days to come.

Tony was Salvadoran, small in stature with piercing dark eyes. With a heavy accent, he stated, "Velcom to mi contree." I soon learned he, too, was a visitor to his country from Houston, where he had moved with his wife and two small children. He had come to serve SHARE as a guide for delegations visiting for the commemoration march and Mass at the UCA, in memory of the murders one year before.

Darkness had enveloped the mountainous terrain as we made the forty-five minute assent from the airport to San Salvador. Tony kept his eyes on the narrow, pothole-filled highway as cars and pickups whizzed past us, some with dim or no taillights. I appreciated the vigilance he devoted to the task of driving, but even so he talked incessantly about his country's social and political conditions. Finally, his interest turned to the reason for my visit and he asked, with an assuming voice, "Are you here for the celebration at the UCA?" And so began my first attempt to explain to a Salvadoran my intention to live for sixteen days with the people in the Cantón El Tablón. His wide-eyed response was, "Why?"

Ultimately he expressed some appreciation for the intent of my visit to the country but seemed surprised I knew so little about the country's history. And he was correct in his suggestion that I would not understand the life of poverty in a vacuum of knowledge about the war and the violence advanced against the poor by the Right Wing Arena Party. He went on in some detail about the martyrdom of Monsignor Oscar Romero, who was shot through the heart by a member of a right-wing death squad while celebrating the Mass at the Divina Providencia Chapel.[3] Once Tony started speaking, he seemed to be full of only what was bad, but what he most obviously thought was necessary, news. He talked about the repressive acts of torture and killings by death squads against anyone who advocated for social need or change. And he punctuated it with the commemoration that would happen on the sixteenth to remember the six Jesuits and two women who were martyred on that date a year earlier[4]. I did not enjoy his description of how the military literally blew out the brains of the Jesuits, so that they lay next to their own broken and shattered skulls. But there was something about the way that he told it that I could tell he knew I was far too naïve about Salvadoran

---

[3] Monsignor Oscar Romero was martyred on March 24,, 1980 at the Divina Providencia Cancer Hospital chapel.

[4] Six Jesuit professors, their housekeeper, and her daughter were martyred at the University of Central America. On November 16, 1989, The six--Ignacio Ellacuria, Segundo Montes, Ignacio Martin-Baro, Joaquin Lopez y Lopez, Juan Ramon Moreno, and Amado Lopez--were murdered by the Salvadoran military on the campus of the University of Central America (UCA) in San Salvador, El Salvador. The housekeeper, Elba Ramos, and her daughter, Celia Marisela Ramos, were murdered there as well. The Jesuits were labeled subversives by the Salvadoran government for speaking out against the oppressive socioeconomic structure of Salvadoran society. Their assassinations were ordered for their unwavering defense of the poor. The Jesuits were six of more than 70,000 victims who died in El Salvador's civil war, which raged in the 1980s and early 1990s. The vast majority of these victims were civilians killed by El Salvador's armed forces and paramilitary death squads. The death of the Jesuits brought international outrage and condemnation upon the Salvadoran government and pressured them to negotiate an end to their country's civil war.

history, and as though his telling the gruesome details of the murders would put it all in perspective for me. His timing was bad. I was not prepared to hear these grisly details and, in fact, I was simply too tired to absorb the full weight of his educative diatribe. That time would come later. It was too much, much too much, too soon, too ugly, and too sad to absorb.

The Next Nine Days

Church bells from the nearby Ceiba de Guadalupe Parish awoke me early from what had been a fitful dream-filled sleep. Diesel fumes from buses screeching to a stop and roaring off with their loads of passengers punctuated the early morning and made continued sleep impossible. Memory of a dream

This rose garden is a memorial on the site where the 6 Jesuit Priests, their housekeeper and her daughter were murdered. It was planted by the housekeeper's husband who discovered the bodies.

lingered as I prepared myself for my first day on Salvadoran soil. The dream was simple but haunting. I was on the first step of a long flight of concrete stairs that descended into an endless, black depth. I could not help sense the note of similarity of the symbols with my own descent into the unknown in the coming days.

I had been the only occupant to sleep in a classroom at the Emilie Junior High School that had been converted into a dormitory for the influx of foreigners coming to the Jesuit commemoration. The aloneness I felt punctuated each solitary moment. Next to the classroom was a chapel. It was obvious there was no separation of church and state issues here. In the chapel I found a half-burnt candle that I used for morning prayer. Slowly, the flaring flame diminished into a barely visible light in a pool of melted candle wax. Even that waning flame was a lingering reminder of the stairs dream, the growing darkness and aloneness that I felt in this strange land. The only thing that seemed to emerge from the darkness was a nagging question that repeated itself over and over in my consciousness, a thought that would be repeated in the days ahead, *"What am I doing here? What am I to do here?"*

When Tony dropped me off at the school the night before, he pointed to a stand-alone building next to the school and said, "That building just west of the main structure is the cafeteria where you will have breakfast." I was ready for my morning meal as I had not eaten since I was on the plane the day before. The thought of food gave pause for a moment to the growing surrealism of the experience so far, but the moment passed, as I exited the school and made my way over to the cafeteria. Then, peering over at that stand-alone building, I recall Tony telling me was WEST of the school, I saw the sun rising. It added to my apprehension. Never in all my life had I been confused about directions. All my life the sun came up in the east. Now the growing surrealism consumed the totality of my being. My decent-and-in-order life was entering a different reality where decency is limited, and disorder thrives in a black hole of human-made misery of violent poverty. There, over a city where perverted political and social agendas prosper, a wounded God cries and prays, *"If only this day you knew the things that make for peace."* Lu. 19.42. The very core of creation as I knew it had begun to weep. In this country where nothing seems normal, where planes are greeted by military escort, toilets are reminders of childhood outhouse experiences, people have their brains blown out for speaking their mind and a monsignor who was sympathetic to the plight of the poor was murdered while saying Mass. Then too, the sun comes up in the west!

I entered the cafeteria with hopes of finding someone with whom I could share a conversation in English. There was no one among the few people having breakfast. Food was slim pickings but plentiful, and I was grateful for my breakfast of red beans, eggs, and tortillas. I washed it down with sweet, black coffee and then went to sit on a rock in front of the school where Tony was to pick me up. He arrived late in his old but well-maintained red Toyota pickup. On the beginning of my first full day, I experienced two cultural realities of El Salvador--beans for breakfast and no one is ever on time.

The altar at Divina Providincia.

Tony's "Buenos Dias" and toothy grin broke into the aloneness I had been feeling and I was grateful to be able to talk with someone. He suggested that the next day I wait behind the fence that surrounds the school. It was a reminder of what he had told me the night before when he dropped me off: "Be careful and don't wander away from the school." He went on to say, "Not everyone is friendly, and a casual stroll can be dangerous, especially for a lone gringo."

The heavy morning traffic polluted the air with a heavy haze and caused frequent delays in our movement. Finally we reached our first stop, the Divina Providencia. It is the Cancer Hospital located in a middle-class neighborhood, where Monsignor Oscar Romero lived, and where he died. We parked in the lot next to the morgue and Tony ushered me toward the chapel. Tony, with sadness in his voice, asked rhetorically how someone could live with himself after shooting a priest through the heart while he was celebrating Mass as they had Monsignor Romero. His death happened on March 24, 1980. The service began at 6 p.m. He had been receiving death threats all day and the nuns had asked him, begged him, not to do the Mass.

His words from previous weeks and months indicated he knew he would be killed. *"If God accepts the sacrifice of my life, may my death be for the freedom of my people ... A bishop will die, but the Church of God, which is the people, will never perish."* (These words were taken from an interview a couple of weeks before his assassination.)

The final homily of Archbishop Romero was spoken in a Mass he performed at the request of Jorge Pinto, the publisher and editor of *"El Indepente,"* a weekly newspaper that was one of the few voices for justice and human rights in El Salvador. It was the first anniversary Mass for Pinto's mother, Sara Meardi de Pinto. Romero based his homily on the John 12. 23-26:

> *The hour has come for the Son of Man to be glorified. Unless a grain of wheat falls to the earth and dies, it remains only a single grain; but if it dies, it will yield a rich harvest. Whoever loves his life will lose it; those who hate their own life in this world will keep it in the life to come. Anyone who would serve me must follow me, for wherever I am, my servant will be there too.*

In his homily, Romero reflected on the noble spirit of Sara Meardi de Pinto, and how she had put all her educated upbringing, her graciousness, at the service of a cause that is so important: the true liberation of all of El Salvador's people:

> *"We should take to ourselves her message that every Christian ought to want to live intensely. You hear in Christ's gospel that one must not love oneself so much so as to avoid getting involved in the risks of life that history demands of us, and that those who try to fend off the danger will lose their lives, while those, who out of love for Christ ,give themselves to the service of others, will live. Life is the grain of wheat that dies,*

but only apparently. If it does not die, it remains alone. The harvest comes about only because it dies, allowing itself to be sacrificed to the earth and destroyed. Only by undoing itself does it produce the harvest."

His words became a self-fulfilling prophecy. Romero could only hold on to the slimmest of hopes that he would die that day. But the darkness prevailed and a death squad had been dispatched to eliminate the voice of reason and love from a society filled with repression and hate. He had committed the unforgivable sin, as far as the Arena Right wing party was concerned. His constant railing against the war and repression, and the unjust practices of the government and military against the poor had sown seeds of hate against the monsignor. But his ultimate challenge to injustice came the day before his murder. In his homily at the cathedral, broadcast on the public airways so everyone could hear, he had called for the military to lay down their arms and to stop killing their own brothers and sisters. *"Before an order to kill that a man may give, the law of God must prevail that says: Thou shalt not kill! No soldier is obliged to obey an order against the law of God."* (Quote from Romero's last Sunday sermon.)

At 6:15 p.m. Monsignor Romero finished his homily and moved behind the communion table to prepare the elements for communion. *"May this Body immolated and this Blood sacrificed for humankind nourish us also, that we may give our body and our blood over to suffering and pain, like Christ--not for self, but to give harvests of peace and justice to our people."* (Words uttered seconds before a gunshot pierced his heart as he prepared to consecrate the Eucharist.)

It was to be the day of the crucifixion of Oscar Romero. The bullet came from a marksman who had positioned himself outside with a view of the altar through the double doors of the chapel. In the instant that the bullet struck, the cup of the sacrament was spilled; the Monsignor gripped the tablecloth covering the altar and fell to the marble floor. In the passage of those moments, his blood mixed with the contents of the consecrated cup, the blood of Christ. Monsignor Romero's murder officially marks the beginning of El Salvador's twelve years long civil war for many of the Salvadoran people. It also began the procession from martyrdom to sainthood for the archbishop whom everyone either loved or hated, Saint Romero.

Tony left me in the chapel and said to spend as much time as I wanted. I stood at the altar where the monsignor celebrated, and was murdered. The double doors in the back, which were the entrance to the sanctuary, were open, just as they had been the night of his murder. How could he not see the rifle barrel aimed at him that night? How could he not be suspicious of the red Volkswagen that was right outside under the tree on the other side of the street? How could he not be more careful in protecting himself? As I stood there frozen in place, my mind raced. I felt both nauseated and ashamed of the part my own nation played in this travesty. Tony had told me on the way to the Divina Providencia that the U.S. government provided the money that allowed death squads to kill people like Monsignor Romero and all the rest of their victims. One to two million dollars a day provided by a generous government of the United States, supposedly under the guise of preventing the spread of Communism, but more likely to insure the smothering of dissent and protest in the face of injustice. Standing in that place, the truth of that support took on meaning that words by themselves can never communicate. My tax dollars killed the monsignor and continued to kill all who resisted the decades of repression against the poor and the advocates of social change.

From the altar, I moved to a pew to clear my mind and still my soul. Scriptural injunctions filled the moment. *Let justice roll down like waters and righteousness like an ever flowing stream"* and *"…if someone strikes you on the right cheek, turn to him the other also."* My thoughts were both contradictory and condemnatory. Truly, the monsignor had lived those moments of wisdom. He had insisted on justice and righteousness for the repressed and he did it consistently with a turn-the-other-cheek posture. And he knew. He knew that the time would arrive when they would murder him to silence him. Gradually, my soul became still, and I sensed a calm that always descends when I visit the chapel at the Divina Providencia, even to this day. That is where I go to renew my soul and spirit when I am in San Salvador. And that day, my first in a series of painful encounters, I learned how the power of spiritual presence, the memory of the presence of Romero, could calm the soul. It was time to go, and as I slowly moved toward the double doors that are the main entrance to the chapel, my mind filled with vision, a reminder of my dream the previous night, of a long stairway, descending into a black abyss. I had taken my first step down.

The rest of the day was insignificant. We spent what was left of the morning planning transportation and other details for a delegation from Pennsylvania with whom I would spend the next eight days. They were to arrive the next day and would sleep in the same school where I slept. After a lunch of pupusas, a cheese-filled tortilla that is El Salvador's staple food, and Coke, I was weighed down with exhaustion. Tony took me back to the school to rest. I collapsed into my bed and almost immediately fell into a deep sleep. When I awoke it was dark. Everything was silent and I looked at the clock on the wall illuminated by dim light in the street. It read 3 a.m. I had slept thirteen hours. I lay there a long time before drifting off to sleep again. As I did, I sensed emptiness of spirit that brought to mind again the question, *"What am I doing here?"*

I awoke before the bells of the church rang, before the sun was up, before the buses fouled the air with diesel smoke. But there was the noise of trucks, many trucks. I peered into the dawning of day from the front door of the school to see a caravan of army trucks carrying soldiers. Tony told me later in the day that November, 1989, one year earlier, the FMLN revolutionaries had made an offensive against San Salvador. They had brought the war to the city to refute the suggestion by government powers that the revolutionaries were nothing more than a band of drug-running delinquents. The anniversary of that offensive along with the first anniversary of the murder of the six Jesuits, their housekeeper and her daughter put everyone on edge. He said that the army was on the move to set up defense against another such attack.

The tense nature of the life of the people took on a personal significance. After preparing for the day, I went to a well-worn bench, behind the fence surrounding the school as instructed, to wait for Tony. For an hour and a half, I watched people who were going about their day. The bus stop was full of people many of them who stood alone. Those who were together said little to one another and when they did speak, they talked in low tones as though not to attract attention. I remembered that Tony he had told me to be subdued and to not attract attention to myself. When I did speak, I was to be casual and quiet. "Eyes and ears are everywhere," he said. Here was proof before my very eyes that the entire society lived on edge so as to not attract attention to themselves.

Tony eased his pickup toward the curb where I was sitting behind the fence. He nodded his approval and motioned me to get in the pickup. He made sure I had my passport with me and said I would most likely need it before the week was over. On the outskirts of San Salvador, we parked behind a waiting empty bus that was transportation for the delegation from Pennsylvania that would arrive within an hour. In caravan, we headed for the airport to meet them, and as we rounded a curve a few miles outside of the city, I could see that traffic backed up for a good distance. He said it most likely was a military checkpoint and as we neared, I could see a bus stopped on the side of the highway. The anguished and fearful faces of women left inside the bus to be interrogated spoke volumes of the tension such stops invoked in their hearts. All the men had been ushered outside, their hands up against the bus, waiting their turn for interrogation. "That is why you needed your passport," he said, "and most likely you will be involved with a military check stop before your trip is over."

He was correct. I spent the rest of the time before going to El Tablón with the delegation from Pennsylvania. One day we visited the Center for International Solidarity (CIS), an organization dedicated to justice for the pueblos of El Salvador. We were all given CIS brochures. Later that day we traveled to an isolated site near Costa del Sol, which is an affluent beach area on the Pacific coast of El Salvador. The purpose was to visit the site where four American church women, Jean Donovan, Ita Ford, Maura Clarke, and Dot or Dorothy Kazel (three nuns and a social worker) had been murdered by death squads on December 2, 1980. What follows is an accurate account of their murders.

In the afternoon of December 2, Jean Donovan and Dorothy Kazel picked up two Maryknoll missionary sisters, Maura Clarke and Ita Ford, from the airport after the pair arrived from attending a Maryknoll conference in Managua, Nicaragua. They were under surveillance by a National Guardsman at the time, who phoned his

commander for orders. Acting on orders from their commander, five National Guard members changed into plain clothes and continued to stake out the airport. The five members of the National Guard of El Salvador, out of uniform, stopped the vehicle the sisters were driving after they left the airport. Donovan and the three sisters were taken to a relatively isolated spot, where they were beaten, raped, and murdered by the soldiers.

At about 10 p.m. on Tuesday, December 2, three hours after Donovan and Kazel picked up Clarke and Ford, local peasants had seen the sisters' white van drive to an isolated spot and then heard machine-gun fire followed by single shots. They saw five men flee the scene in the white van, with the lights on and the radio blaring. The van would be found later that night, on fire at the side of the airport road.

Early the next morning, Wednesday, December 3, they found the bodies of the four women, and were told by local authorities—a judge, three members of the civil guard, and two commanders—to bury the women in a common grave in a nearby field. Four of the local men did so, but informed their parish priest, and the news reached the local bishop and the U.S. Ambassador to El Salvador, Robert White, the same day.

The shallow grave was exhumed the next day, Thursday, December 4, in front of fifteen reporters, Sisters Alexander and Dorsey, and several missioners, and Ambassador White. Donovan's body was the first removed; then Kazel's; then Clarke's; and last, Ford's. The next day, a Mass of the Resurrection was said by the bishop, Arturo Rivera y Damas. On Saturday, December 6, the bodies of Jean Donovan and Dorothy Kazel were flown out for burial, Donovan to her parents' town of Sarasota, Florida, and Kazel to her hometown of Cleveland, Ohio. The bodies of the Maryknoll sisters, Clarke and Ford, were not repatriated and were buried in Chalatenango. The U.S. State Department charged the Donovans $3,500 for the return of their daughter's body.[5]

---

5   Account taken from Wikipedia, the free encyclopedia.

Photo of the four slain women that hangs at the memorial chapel erected in their honor

As we turned off the highway to the airport onto the coastal highway known as El Litoral, we were stopped at a military checkpoint. Of course, we were asked for passports and the van we were riding in was searched. CIS brochures were the only evidence of liberal minds, but that was sufficient for the checkpoint personnel to consider the group Communist supporters. We were detained for what seemed like an hour, but in the end, we were let go with the warning to respect the lives and laws of El Salvador. It seemed rather an absurdity, since the oligarchy that these soldiers protect, did not. It brings to mind the words once spoken by Mohandas Gandhi when asked British Journalist what he thought of western civilization. Gandhi replied, *"I think it is would be good idea."*

We turned off the blacktop full of potholes onto a dirt road on the edge of the pueblo where the four women had been murdered. Within minutes, we arrived at the massacre site. Today there is a chapel and monument on the site where the four American women were killed. In 1990 when we made the visit to the site, there was not even a marker to indicate the martyrdom of the women had happened there. An eerie silence punctuated our arrival. There was not a soul in sight, and I could not help but sense the wrenching fear the women must have felt that dreadful night, on the forty-five minute drive from the site of their abduction just outside the airport to that spot. There could have been no doubt in their minds that they were about to die. After all, they had witnessed it many times before, among the people for whom they cared and to whom they ministered. But first two of them were raped. The U.S. Ambassador to the United Nations at the time, Jean Kirkpatrick, was quoted on December 16, 1980, about the matter: *"I don't think the government (of El Salvador) was responsible. The nuns were not just nuns; the nuns were political activists. We ought to be a little more clear-cut about this than we usually are. They were political activists on behalf of the Frente, and somebody who is using violence to oppose the Frente killed them."* [6]

Of course, it was a lie, accompanying so many lies told by representative of the U.S. both to the world and to its own citizens. Like this one by Secretary of State Alexander Haig, when he testified as follows before the Foreign Affairs Committee of the House of Representatives: *"I would like to suggest to you that some of the investigations would lead one to believe that perhaps the vehicle that the nuns were riding in may have tried to run a roadblock or may have accidentally been perceived to have been doing so, and there may have been an exchange of fire."* [7]

Note Haig's wording in his defense of the women's murders: *"I would like to suggest,.. [they] may have tried to run a roadblock."*

Haig knew, and today the entire world knows, that they were nothing more than women who felt the need to help the poor of their respective parishes in La Libertad and Chalatenango to learn how to read and write, sew, and grow a garden. But such support of the poor was seen as support to the revolutionary FMLN and an insult to the ruling Conservative party. Death squads were used to make that point.

As we sat at the martyr site in silence, I felt the same nausea I had felt before when I visited the site of Monsignor Romero's murder,

---

6 Tampa Tribune, 25 December 1980, pp. 23A and 24A, col. 1.
7 See Foreign Assistance Legislation for Fiscal Year 1982: Hearings before the House Committee on Foreign Affairs, 97th Congress, First Session 163, 1981.

accompanied by a deepening anger. It was more and more apparent how the financial support from the U.S. to the Salvadoran army and death squads was the cause of death to the innocent. I could not even imagine the fear and ultimately the resignation to death the four women must have felt that dark night in December, 1980. I wondered silently how men come to be able to commit such gruesome torture of the innocent, men who perhaps have family, wives, or daughters, whose lives they cherish. On the way back to San Salvador, the bus was silent. No one spoke of the visit we just made to a macabre site of torture. I closed my eyes and a dark chasm came to my mind's eye, with the steps descending. One more step down…to where…to what?

In the ensuing days leading up to my journey to El Tablón, I learned about the country's poverty in the midst of the fear and intimidation sustained by the government. Women stood at stoplights with children in arms, begging for a few centavos from the passing motorists. There were street children, ages as young as five years old and without adult support, begging for food. Hungry hands of the poor quickly snatched food left on plates when we ate in outdoor restaurants. My heart ached and the biblical cry of the oppressed grew loud and angry. Jesus' injunction to feed the hungry and clothe the naked took on meaning far beyond any understanding I had before. And the seeming impossibility of making a difference in that social reality tortured my mind. On reflection from the present, it is clear that knowledge and understanding can evolve out of the heartbreak that precedes it. The only way in which feeding the hungry can become a priority is when it grows beyond the perfunctory crumbs falling from the tables of the privileged.

I attended the UCA martyr march or November 16. It was an experience that gave me a taste of the tense fear and stark anger that drove the poor of El Salvador. It began at the Liberty Park across from the National Cathedral and we walked five kilometers to the university, where the Jesuits and women had been martyred one year earlier. Angry young leaders of the march chanted slogans of a people's (FMLN) victory and kerosene fueled flares lighted the way, which was lined with Salvadoran citizens and M-16 armed Salvadoran soldiers.

I marched with thousands, yet I felt alone. I sensed a union with a culture I did not know or understand, and the need for justice permeated the collective consciousness of the marchers. *"El pueblo unido..."* ("the pueblo united will never be defeated") echoed over and over and the anger of the army personnel along the way became more and more obvious. Their M-16s were elevated, and their faces expressed hatred of those in the march. The two sides were clearly defined. The large crowd of protestors snaked its way through the dark streets empty of cars. The steady chant of the marchers and the flaring flames of kerosene-fueled torches mesmerized me with awe and wonder that was underscored by fear. I considered the injunction of my parents to never point a gun at anyone, loaded or unloaded. I was certain that the soldiers lining the street not only had loaded M-16s but also would love the opportunity to use them. Anger and confusion have a way of bringing tragedy. It could happen, I thought. But it didn't. I was never so glad to see the end of a demonstration. We arrived at the UCA, and the Mass began in the large parking lot setup with chairs and stage for the event.

In the safety of that moment, my emotions ran high. I felt deeply saddened, worried, and ignorant all together in one tightly-wound emotional bundle. But more, what was the meaning of all this? What was I doing here? It is easy to look back two decades later and smile at that moment. But at the time of that moment nothing made sense. In the middle of a Mass spoken in Spanish, I paused for my own time with God. I remember the prayer to this day. *"Give me understanding. Give me wisdom. Give me peace of mind."* The prayer was answered… in God's time… little by little…and not fully until years later. *"When I was a child, I spoke like a child, I thought like a child, I reasoned like a child; but when I put aside my childish ways, I began to see as an adult"*. (1 Cor. 13.11)

Chapter 2

Sixteen Days of Heartbreak

"The young fox dashed across the frozen lake, thus getting his tail wet. The old, wiser, fox steps and listens, steps and listens, and crosses the lake dry."
I Ching

Tony, my guide for the first ten days of the journey, had done an excellent job of showing me Third World poverty and educating me of its ugly and consuming violence. In the experience I could not help but note that sadness is poverty's common denominator, regardless of the location, whether First World or Third World. Yet, I felt a definable distinction in poverty between the two worlds. Organized violence is the factor that makes Third World poverty distinct from poverty in First World nations. The violence is organized and it is brutal. It is a troubling cruelty and, in the case of El Salvador, permitted and encouraged in the unholy alliance between the Salvadoran and U.S. governments, which provided the financial and political support to carry out a strategy of violent repression.

The U.S. strategists defended the support as the tactic of "low-intensity conflict" needed to fight Communist aggression in the Central American region. This was a lame but necessary excuse forwarded to preserve the politics of control fueled by the sweet, putrid smell of death. [8]

---

[8] A foreign policy strategy adopted by the U.S. in the wake of the Vietnam defeat

At the end of the first ten days of my heartbreak journey, I had learned a great deal about Salvadoran poverty. But my learning experience about Third World poverty would have been incomplete without becoming familiar with the menacing violence and intimidation that drives the survival instincts of the poor of the nation. Until I had experienced their poverty in an upfront and personal way, I knew only the view of the academic observer, but nothing as a participant by which the spirit can speak directly with the heart. It was the awareness of this intimidating fear, instilled by the brutal violence of war and death squads that torture, which broke my heart that ultimately opened a door in my dream. I now remembered what I had known all along was behind it, at the bottom of the long dark descending stairs. There in El Tablón violence from north met violence from south and bonded in spirit in a mutual revelation that compelled me on this justice driven faith journey.

It is the factor of violence prevalent in their lives that makes Salvadoran poverty dissimilar from U.S. poverty. And it was the emotional ingredient that changed my "ugly American" quest of learning about poverty into a spiritual journey of experiencing poverty's pain. It became a life-changing experience driven by a quest for justice in the land of El Salvador, where the power of the American influence and violent strategies had become the authority over the destiny of the Salvadoran poor. It was the awareness of this intimidating fear, instilled by brutal violence, which not only broke my heart, but also stirred something within me, long forgotten, hidden decades ago in the psyche of a six-year-old, brutalized boy. The pain of it began to rise in me even before that night in El Tablón. I sensed something, I knew not what, but ultimately it would be the experience that bonded me with the Salvadoran quest for justice.

---

to use fear tactics and intimidation with trained death squads. Ivan Molloy, in his book, "Rolling Back the Revolution: The Emergence of Low-Intensity Conflict" does an excellent job of explaining the philosophy behind the strategy and how it works. He analyzes the strategy behind low-intensity conflict (LIC) and the broad emergence of its use particularly under the Reagan administration. This method would avoid the pitfalls of the historic backlash resulting from cases of direct intervention, re: Vietnam. LIC was developed to covertly attack revolutionary governments (usually Marxist), considered threatening to national interests.

Tony handed me off to Mike Hoffman at the commemoration for the Jesuit professors and two women at the University of Central America. He was the on-the-ground activist for SHARE Foundation, who would coordinate the rest of my trip. First he asked me about my visa--how many days had they given me at immigration when I entered the country? "Thirty days," I said. "No way," he said. At the Chicago Embassy, that is what they stamped in my passport. He opened my passport and there was the official declaration of twelve days when I had entered the country. I had been in the country for eleven. Mike was surprisingly calm and counseled me on the matter, but neglected to help me understand the true significance of the issue. He said I had to make a choice. I could go to the immigration office the next day and ask for an extension to my visa. But there was little chance for an extension. "Or, on the other hand," Mike said, "You can go ahead on to El Tablón and wait to deal with it when you return to San Salvador from there." I did not know exactly the impact of Mike's statement when he said, "I could deal with the visa issue when I returned from El Tablón," and I did not wish to trouble myself with asking for details at that moment. At this step of the journey, ignorance was bliss. I made my decision. I would go forward as planned. Mike also informed me that translators were unavailable for all the days of my stay in El Tablón. John Donaghy, a campus minister at Iowa State University in Ames, would go with me the next day and stay for three days. Eleven days later, Josie, another staff person with SHARE Foundation, would arrive in the cantón to translate for the final two days of my stay. It felt a little unsettling that I would be there alone without capability of communicating with the people, but not enough that I wanted to abandon my journey to educate myself about Third World poverty.

We traveled by pickup truck, leaving for El Tablón the next morning at 2:30 a.m. Under the eerie translucent light of a gasoline station, we loaded our luggage into the pickup and climbed aboard. It was to be the first of many rides for me in the back of a pickup in the coming years of my Salvadoran travel. The coolness of the early morning made me glad I had packed a jacket, as the breeze of the ride was cold upon the face. The dim glow from the street lights created eerie shadows across the street. There were no other cars on the road, and it was as though we were sole survivors of the land. The road was rutted and pot-holed and, as we left the city limits, the darkness of the moonless night enveloped us into the great unknown that lay ahead. When we had boarded the pickup, the driver had some advice for us. He had said he hoped we could make it without going through a military checkpoint, and quickly added that this early in the morning, it was unlikely we would encounter one. But if we did, he said, we would suffer an interrogation as to why we were traveling so early in the morning. "If this happens," he said, "let me do the talking." It struck me as funny, given my inability to speak the language. I wouldn't be able to speak with the military even if they demanded it.

The one hundred kilometer trip from San Salvador to Berlin took about three hours. My anxiety over what the driver had said about the improbable stop at a military checkpoint increased with each pueblo through which we passed. I know he said it was improbable, but the very fact he mentioned it said to me it was possible. I reminisced about home and the ease and comforts and freedom of travel. The aromas of the countryside were of wood burning and of a sweet, almost rancid odor I would later learn was of coffee being processed. Barking dogs announced our coming and going to the shuttered shacks that dotted the way. I had entered a second phase of my trip.

We turned off the Pan American Highway at the pueblo Mercedes Urmana for the final six kilometers up the mountain to the pueblo of Berlin. By that time there were a few vehicles on the road; mostly pickups, loaded with people on their way to cut coffee. We passed through Berlin as it was awakening to a new day. I felt a bit of relief as we drove onto the rutted, dirt roads of the mountainside that connected the cantóns of the countryside with the pueblo. We would make it the whole way without a military interrogation. I cannot deny the deep sense of relief in which I wallowed.

Soon we were on a steep incline, and there was little doubt that the mountain road was too much for the two-wheel drive pickup. Tires made a shrill noise on the packed dry volcanic earth as the driver gunned the engine to move us beyond the peak that would lead to El Tablón in the valley below. Suddenly he stopped trying, and all became silent around us. Then he spoke the words I dreaded, "Sorry, guys. We can't go any further. You have to continue on foot." There was a small hut nearby, and he walked causally but with caution to the dark home. After a long and anxious wait, a man peeked out from a crack in the door. It was apparent that he was as anxious about an early morning intrusion as we were about making one. He and the driver talked for a few minutes and, after hearing the story, he volunteered to be our guide to the cantón. We unloaded the suitcases and watched the small pickup that had carried us to this place in the wilderness disappear over the hill. There was no turning back now.

We walked a few hundred yards on the road and then veered off onto a very steep footpath. Our volunteer guide suggested we leave the suitcases at a hut near where we had exited the road. He knew the people who lived there and someone from the cantón could return later to collect them for us, he said. It would make the walk ahead much easier. I had to trust him, although, I must confess, I doubted I would ever see my suitcase again.

We walked--I should say I stumbled--and slid over the pea-gravel on the steep mountain path, for an hour or so. We came to an abandoned school, and our guide announced we had arrived in El Tablón. But, it was another half-hour walk to the end of the narrow cantón before we came to the hut of Carmen, who would be the hostess. As we approached the dirt yard of her home, several members of the community greeted us. They were kind and full of smiles. A man in a large cowboy hat handed me an orange that had been cut into two pieces. Never had I tasted such a sweet orange. Our kind guide told the men assembled about the suitcases, and a small group immediately left to retrieve them for us. I felt very grateful and warmly welcomed by the hospitality of what would be my home for the next sixteen days.

Life in El Tablón

Carmen's house had a cement floor and appeared to be the most comfortable home in the cantón. Obviously, that was one of the reasons it had been chosen as the place where the gringo would live while visiting. It was the last home in the long cantón, making it the most isolated and least likely to be discovered by the military. Two things immediately caught my attention: a man with a green bandana around his neck and carrying a rifle and three women making hundreds of tortillas. The man who was armed was a member of the revolutionaries who were fighting for the rights and needs of the poor of the land.

I spent the rest of my morning getting oriented to my new surroundings. A large tree shaded much of the dirt area in front of the house. There was an embankment to climb up from the road in order to get to the house. And all traffic, which was either by foot or animal, could be seen for some distance. Later I learned a key factor for choosing Carmen's home for my stay was that if the military came, it would be known well in advance. And if I was found there by the military, I also learned later, everyone would surround me and they would have to take everyone in order to get to me. In my ignorance, I had no fear, nor did I understand the risk being taken on my behalf by these simple brave people, who were constantly afraid for my safety. Sometimes ignorance truly is bliss..

Sisters carrying water from the river.

Up to that point of the trip, I had seen and heard about poverty. Now I was living in the midst of it. The toilet was the field behind the house. The bath was a small spring about a twenty-minute walk away, which was also the place where cantaros (jugs) were filled with water for the homes and where women took the laundry to be washed on the rocks near the spring. Carmen fixed me a breakfast of eggs and red beans. Lunch was the same, and dinner, that's right, the same. The next day Carmen disappeared for the morning and when she returned she had a small roast. She had walked to the market in Berlin to buy special food for me. It was painfully humbling, as she cut slabs of meat for my lunch that day and gave me white bread instead of the usual tortilla. The visiting gringo would have only the best hospitality possible for her to offer. With John's help translating, I was able to communicate that everyone should have meat to eat, and I wanted to eat only what they had themselves. The women who came daily to make the tortillas smiled when I suggested that, and I sensed an appreciation for my attitude and desire to know their lives in the poverty they lived. I confess, however, that by the time I left the cantón, two weeks later, I was truly glad that I could have a meal that did not include eggs or beans.

Bedtime comes early in a cantón. Since there is no electricity, and it gets dark by 6:30 p.m., there is not a great deal that can be accomplished after nightfall. There were seven of us in the one room home: Carmen, her three children (Walter, Vilma, and Billy), John and I. Her husband and eldest son were fighting with the revolutionary force in another part of the country. The door was bolted, and a large timber slid into place, to prevent easy entry by the military if they showed up in the middle of the night. It had happened before and Carmen had been threatened with death across an M-16 rifle barrel pointed at her head. Another generous gift they provided me was a folding cot with woven cords instead of canvas to sleep on. And Carmen kept a candle burning through the night to provide dim lighting. Soon, the reason for the candle became apparent. Her concern was that the rats in the rafters not drop down and bite the children. It was mine as well, as I could hear the vermin scuttling about above my bed, and I feared one would fall on me during the night. Sleep was fitful, to say the least.

I woke in the morning with a few welts on my right side, which is the side I sleep on the most. There were bugs of some kind in my bed. By the time I was to leave for my return to San Salvador, my right side was a rash of bites. One morning at the spring, when I was bathing, a FMLN doctor noticed the red welts. She sent an aide to the camp to bring some kind of cream, and gave me a shot to ease the itching. Desperately needed medicine for the revolutionaries was used on me that morning. It was another humbling indication of the hospitality the community offered to me.

When John left three days into my stay, it began eleven days without human conversation. My morning routine consisted of helping Vilma, Carmen's daughter, sweep the chicken droppings from the previous night that were deposited on the hard dirt in front of the house. I accompanied Carmen to the spring to retrieve water, but it was she, not I, who had the strength to carry the fifty- pound cantaro of water from the spring back to the house. After breakfast I spent the rest of the morning sitting under the large tree writing my reflections of what I saw in the life of poverty I was experiencing. By 9 a.m., like clockwork, a small contingent of revolutionaries dressed in green appeared from the heavy green foliage on the perimeter of the yard to carry hundreds of tortillas made by the three women. What I didn't know but soon learned was that the tortillas were for the revolutionaries at their encampment nearby. At first, they eyed me with some suspicion. I am sure they wondered why a gringo, who could not speak the language, would come for such a visit. One day, the small contingent stopped where I was sitting with my pen and pad and said something to me. I did not know what they said, but I could tell from their facial expressions and smiles that I had been accepted as a non-threatening presence for them and the people of the cantón. From that time on, more and more of the FMLN came to Carmen's home and occasionally a few of them would sit under the tree with me, even though we were unable communicate verbally. It gave me a sense of security, as it had become quite apparent that a war was raging, and it was common to hear distant gunfire during the day and night. It was a rather contradictory comfort for my pacifist soul to know that these armed revolutionaries were close by and that they considered me a friendly presence.

I yearned for news from the outside world. While there was none I could understand, the cantón residents had their own yearning to know how the war was going. Their source for information came through Radio Vinceremos in daily noon and 6 p.m. broadcasts by the booming voice of a man named Santiago that gave the FMLN take on what was happening in the struggle for justice. The battery-operated radio was turned on at the time of the broadcast, with a large number of people gathered to hear the news. Their expressions and exclamations were the signs of victory or defeat. One night after the broadcast, people lingered, looking to the east, which seemed west to me, with some intensity. I stood with them, not knowing what they were awaiting. Then, far out in the distance, a huge fireball rose from the skyline. They cheered! And their cheers were evidence of satisfaction that a well-placed bomb had been victoriously executed.

I began counting the days until my departure. I felt despair at times and anxiously yearned for home. I had experienced the grinding poverty I needed to know. I realized that a week had given me all the experience I needed for a clear understanding, and thus, the information I needed in order to write the promotional materials, which was the genesis of my decision to make the trip in the first place. The bug bites on my body and the rats in the rafters above my head tortured my mind and sleep. I was beginning to feel trapped. I was feeling more than a bit distressed, lacking any language skills to express my despair and no idea at all of the way that would lead me out of the wilderness and back into my comfortable First World life again.

The dream I had some long days ago, with the stairs leading down into a black chasm, recurred, this time several steps down into the darkness below. It was another moment in my life in which I sensed God's design for my life was being discovered. Had I left El Tablón after a few days, it would have served to be nothing more than an information-gathering trip. With each additional step I took, it was becoming clearer to me that I had to know something more, I had to sense a deeper connection to these people and come to own, not just know, how the brutality of poverty weaves itself into human life. Only more time would produce what I needed to experience if I were to clearly discern that to which God was calling me. Experience is the source of spiritual reflection that leads one to a decision, and then to take action. God knew I had to experience more in order that in my understanding of this call might mature to a point of being unforgettably etched into my soul. It is the scars of our old wounds that serve to remind us of our experiences, and how to change our lives in such a way as to shield us from future harm and, hopefully, from being wounded in quite the same way again. In turn, we learn to shield others from the same pain or fate. I could tell that my soul was being wounded by this experience, and that perhaps a call was beginning to take shape. Thus, in this sense, the days wore on.

In spite of the hindrance of language, my relationships with the cantón residents deepened. When Josie, the translator for my final two days in El Tablón, arrived, the trust I had established with the people became the stage for the telling of their stories. It was a painful turning of the page in my journal when Josie was there to translate the violence my new friends had experienced in massacres some years before. They had come to El Tablón as a place to resettle and begin life anew.

Two evenings before my departure from the cantón, several women, Josie, and I gathered in Carmen's kitchen, which was an attached hut to her home. They wanted the outside world to hear of the violence they and thousands of others had experienced. I was to be their conduit for communication of that violence to the outside world. Dim light, provided by the candles they had lit, accentuated sad faces that prepared to remember their time spent in hell as they were on the run from the Salvadoran military. It was in the early to mid-1980s that the military had adopted a strategy, likely on the advice of U.S. military intelligence and, to my mind, spawned of an evil incomprehensible to most people of conscience. The philosophy of it was that by killing the cantón populations, the FMLN would lack a support base to continue the revolution. Their cantón had been a victim of that strategy. Each one told their horror story, and each one was the same. The names were different, their children's ages were different, but the terror they expressed, that pervaded the hearts and souls of those who ran for their lives, was one and the same.

Carmen was the most expressive. She told how the military came one morning and began killing everyone. People ran to escape the massacre. Eventually, those whose lives were spared became a group on the run together. They traveled under the cover of night to try to avoid discovery. During the daytime, they hid in the vegetation-filled gullies and caves. They foraged for food and searched for springs or creeks to provide life-giving water. Sometimes the military came dangerously close to their hiding place. She recalled one particular time when they came so close that parents were forced to stifle children's noise by holding their hands over nose and mouth. Sometimes the suffocation was so long it caused unconsciousness of some children. As Carmen told that part of the story, she became particularly emotional. Vilma, her ten-year-old daughter, who had become my companion of sorts, was sitting on my lap. Carmen's tear-filled eyes looked at her daughter and I, at the same time, could feel Vilma's body tensing up as she remembered her own experience of that time which her mother was describing. I felt my throat tightening with sadness, mixed with anger that gave way to nausea, as once again I felt deep shame for the pain caused by my own country and its support of the Salvadoran military. I felt embarrassment that our tax dollars paid for these crimes against humanity. Then a kind of vertigo began to envelop me. I became dizzy, disoriented, and filled with a vague sense of impending danger. All these images of violence, created by the stories of these amazing women, were all rolling together in my mind and were overwhelming it. I began to weep uncontrollably.

Those feelings deepened, perhaps refined, in the day and months to come, as I began to recall a very brutal moment in my younger life, a memory I had buried in my subconscious, still too vague to grasp. It too had involved suffocation, and the memory of it accompanied by some deeper trauma. Ultimately, it put me into a clinical depression from which, with the assistance of therapy, I have since fully recovered. I mention it now only to make note of the thread of association, or commonality if you will, that compelled me to return again and again to live among the persecuted, traumatized people of El Salvador. *"Blessed are those who are persecuted for the sake of goodness, for to them belongs the realm of heaven."* (Mt. 5:10).

Sleep over the past two weeks had been fitful. That last night I did not sleep at all. I felt as though I had taken the final step down into the blackness at the bottom of the stairs from my dream. What was there beyond? Was it to become a new perspective on life, on my life? Was it a tomb, was it resurrection? Would it be the beginning of a new way of perceiving my walk of faith with Jesus? Perhaps that and much more, for as I view that time in retrospect, I have come to realize an entirely new understanding of living the Gospel that grew out of this, my first Salvadoran journey. My journey to heartbreak from that first trip put me on a journey to faith.

On the final full day in El Tablón, after the usual morning routine, I took my same familiar place, my guard post, under the tree to watch the community life. I often dozed between thoughts and reflections, but that day I felt exhausted from the night before and fell into a deep sleep. When I awoke, I noticed several people I had not seen before. I noticed a table from Carmen's home had been brought into the yard and it was filled with sweet-bread. Dead tree branches and logs had been piled high in the center of the open area in front of Carmen's house, and then I heard Josie say there was to be a party in my honor for the visit I made to their canton. By late afternoon, the yard was filled with familiar faces, as well as a number of strangers. A string band had been set up in front of Carmen's house. I had watched all this from my perch under the tree, and the people of El Salvador watched me with smiles. Late in the day the party began.

The people of not only El Tablón, but also other cantóns close by, had come to say thank you to me for making this visit, and to wish me well on my travels back to my home. Josie translated their speeches of gratitude. I was the first person ever to visit them. Then they gave me a basket filled with small sacks of all the agricultural products of their area. I thanked them as best I could and then the band began to play and the bonfire was lit. A large iron kettle of coffee was brewed and sweet bread was plentiful for all. I found myself somewhat amazed to be at a party in the midst of a large group of FMLN soldiers, in essence, the enemies of my country, because they are the enemies of the government of El Salvador. A large number of the revolutionaries were young women with rifles on their backs, who invited me to dance with them. It brought to mind the words of the feminist anarchist Emma Goldman, an American revolutionary in her own right: *"If I can't dance, I don't want to be part of your revolution."* It was a romantic moment that I will forever carry in my heart. I was extremely tired and went to bed by 11 p.m. But the band played on well into the night to celebrate my coming, and to enjoy some time of well-earned recreation.

I left the cantón the next morning. At the appointed 8 a.m. departure time, several people from the cantón gathered to say goodbye. Four women had been chosen to make the four-hour walk with us down the mountain to where Josie and I would catch a bus to San Salvador. I looked at the small crowd that had gathered. I had so much wanted to go home, but now I felt as though I was abandoning my new friends with whom I had not even been able to converse. Several voices at once expressed the Salvadoran "que le via bien." It literally means "go the way of good." To which I replied, with my heart, not my head, from the spirit not my mind, and with some astonishment to myself, "I will be back." Josie translated my feeble promise of return and smiles filled the tired faces of people caught in poverty and war. I didn't know how, but I knew in my heart it was a promise I would keep.

The Final Three Days

Three days remained before my departure from El Salvador. They would prove to be a lifetime in and of themselves. The descent from the cantón down into the valley below was slow going. The women would not hear of me carrying my luggage, which included a large duffle bag and a regular suitcase. We passed the burned-out skeletal remains of a mansion that had been home to rich landowners, feudal lords who had used the poor as slaves to till the soil and raise the crops. Coffee was the primary crop of the higher elevation, but as we descended down to lower elevations, sugar cane and beans were more prevalent. The lush green landscape from the recent rainy season made it seem like walking through a paradise. I did not know until several years later, when discussing the walk with one of the women who accompanied me on the journey that we in fact had twice passed close to death. A snake they had killed, slithering on the path we walked, was a coral snake, a venomous serpent, the bite of which can kill within four hours. But the more ominous threat for them came from the presence of the National Guard soldiers who were encamped near the river. The National Guard was the backbone of death squad operatives, another kind of serpent. I recall that they eyed the large duffle bag one of the women was carrying for me, but let us pass without delay. We arrived at the river and paid a waiting boat a Colón (the currency of the time that was the equivalent of 12.5 cents in American money) to carry us across the rapids to the other side.

We scurried up the riverbank to a well-worn path that led to the Pan American Highway. Within a few minutes, a bus approached and we made hurried goodbyes with the women who had ushered me on to my reentry into civilization. Josie and I climbed into the bus as it lurched forward with the dozen or so passengers it carried. I watched out the back window at the four women, waving goodbye. I could feel my throat constricting as the lump rose in my throat and my eyes began to smart with tears. Only then did I comprehend the depth to which the people of El Tablón had taken up residence in my heart. The moment passed as I was captured by the satisfaction that at last I was on my back to home and to the comforts of my life.

On the trip to San Salvador, I saw the countryside for the first time, as it had been under cover of darkness that I had made my trip to El Tablón sixteen days earlier. The bridge across the Río Lempa was a pontoon crossing. Revolutionaries had blown up the main bridge. We drove through mountains and when the famed San Vicente Mountain came into view, the natural beauty of the Salvadoran landscape was captured in all of its magnificence. The adobe and sapling shacks that dotted the way were a sharp contrast that emphasized even more the permeating poverty of the Salvadoran people.

The monotonous sound of the diesel bus lulled my tired body to sleep and the next thing I knew we were stopped not far from the Terminal Oriente. People groaned as the National Guard unit ordered everyone off the bus. Then, with the point of a finger, they called me to reboard. Josie looked worried and whispered, "Just do whatever they want and if they take you I will follow to make sure we know where you are." I felt nervous when they asked for my passport, as I was sure I was going to be found out now. Now they would know that I didn't have a visa. But they were so curious about what was in the duffle bag that they did nothing more than compare the photo in the passport with my face. With the barrel of an M-16, they poked through my belongings that were nothing more than dirty clothes. They asked me a question and my only response was, "No hablo español." Josie saw the attempt to communicate, and she asked permission to come on board to translate. Then we learned they were searching for guns. The National Guard unit we passed at the river on the way to the bus had radioed ahead that we should be stopped and searched. It was no secret I had been in FMLN-controlled territory for a couple weeks and they were suspicious of my intent. They let us go and I breathed a sigh of relief that they had been so intent on finding contraband of some kind that they failed to check my visa.

Later I asked Josie what we would do to deal with the visa issue I was facing. She replied that she did not know. Then I wondered to myself what Mike Hoffman had meant when he said the night before I left for El Tablón that we would deal with [the visa issue] when I returned from El Tablón to San Salvador.

Mike met us at the bus depot and suggested I come to sleep at his house for the remaining three days of my trip. Rosa, his wife, was in agreement, and being Salvadoran herself, she knew the ordeal I went through by visiting El Tablón for sixteen days. She cooked a typical Salvadoran dinner and then gave me one of her children's beds in which to sleep. The freshly laundered sheets were such a contrast to the experience I had had in El Tablón, and I was grateful there were no bugs to bite me. I went to sleep as soon as I hit the bed and woke twelve hours later staring at a white wall. I was disoriented and for a moment had that feeling of not knowing where I was. It was momentary and as I refocused my thoughts, I was overwhelmed by the memory of the El Tablón experience. I realized that it would take me quite a long time to come to terms with its impact and perhaps my lifetime to explore what lay beyond that door at the bottom of the dark stairs.

There remained but two days before my return to Iowa; all was well and I was eager to make the trip home. When we were having breakfast, a young Salvadoran woman came to Mike and Rosa's home. She conferred with Mike, and I could tell something was up. They came back to the table together and she addressed me in perfect English. "Will you accompany a repopulation caravan of people who had been living on the streets of San Salvador for the past six years?" she asked. She went on to explain that the Cantón La Paz, near the pueblo San Vicente had been massacred several years ago and those who escaped fled to San Salvador. The lack of employment made their lives next to impossible, and they had decided to return to the place of their roots. She explained the presence of gringos on the caravan would make it safer for the Salvadorans. I, along with three other gringos, would accompany them. I felt honored to be able to "do something" in the face of the tragedy the poor lived, and I immediately said, "Yes!" My friends who know me well also know that I am prone to drive through life without the use of my brakes.[9]

---

9   Note: I have ridden with Bob on many occasions, both actually and metaphorically, and am able to testify to the validity of his statement that he really does "drive on occasions without the use of his brakes." Ed.

Mike smiled and Rosa, though happy, expressed reservations. "It could be dangerous if the military decided to take issue with the repopulation," she said. But she could see I was determined and her foreboding words were useless. She packed a small bag with bread and fruit and kissed my cheek as she handed it to me. It was only later that I learned of Rosa's first husband being murdered by a death squad. Her fear for my own safety had deep roots.

I rode with the young woman who had come to ask me to accompany the caravan to CRIPDES.[10] It is an organization that helps communities organize and had put together the resources for thirteen trucks and pickups to carry the people and their meager belongings. Excitement was in the air as the hundred or so refugees climbed into the vehicles to carry them home. I could sense a deep pride among the staff of CRIPDES that they would drive families back to land that was rightfully theirs, where they could farm the land and have beans and tortillas on a regular basis once again.

We rode for two hours without incident. It was only when the caravan veered off the main highway between the pueblos Zacatecoluca and San Vicente onto a narrow and little traveled path did the Salvadoran military make its move. The caravan was stopped in an open field with the San Vicente Mountain looming in the distance. We were a mile from the former homes of those on the caravan, but it might as well have been on the other side of the universe. I felt angry as the families who had been so hopeful about beginning a new life on their own land were told they could not proceed any further. Anyone who did would be shot. Those on the caravan were given free movement to leave but could not go forward. There was a quickly called meeting of the leadership of the caravan, and just as quickly they decided they would not leave. They would negotiate for passage to their land, but it was late and that would have to wait until the next day. Small campfires began to appear for cooking and so the standoff between the poor and the military began.

---

10   CRIPDES is a Salvadoran organization dedicated to the repopulation of people who have been displaced from the land. It also has a wing that focuses on educating people around the issue of justice.

I was given a blanket and told to dig a place into the ground so I would be sleeping below the surface. If there was any gunfire, I would be safer. I had not felt such a threat of violence in my sixteen days in El Tablón and the possibility that I could now be caught in crossfire made me realize more of what Rosa's concern had been regarding my accompanying the caravan. Poverty has a putrid smell, but adding the menace of violence to that smell makes the stench unbearable. I dug an indentation in the earth and lay down on the blanket, feeling as though the possibility of returning to my comfortable home was more remote than before. I felt crushed by the oppression that was the life of the poor of this land. I watched the full moon move across the sky and did not sleep a wink. I thought of home, but I also thought about the remarkable friends I had made in El Tablón. The comforts of First World were never more inviting. The difficulties of Third World were never so overwhelming.

As the sun appeared over the land, I felt relief and gratitude that no gunfire had occurred. People began to mill about, and I could see the groupings of Salvadoran soldiers that constituted the barrier between the people of the caravan and the land they so badly wanted to reclaim. A small group of the leadership from CRIPDES went by Jeep to San Vicente to begin negotiations with the military to allow the caravan to move forward. Another Jeep took me back to San Salvador so I could catch my plane home the next day. The adventure with the caravan had overshadowed my concern about the visa issue. Even though we had escaped gunfire the night before, I knew I could no longer dodge this bullet.

Mike and Rosa drove me to the airport the next morning. A pickup load of their friends followed. They feared I would be taken by the military for interrogation once it was discovered that I did not have a visa, that I, Rev. Robert Cook, was, in fact, an illegal immigrant in El Salvador. They promised to follow to wherever I was taken. I checked in and went up the stairs to the exit from ticketing to the waiting area for boarding. The group that had come to ensure my whereabouts in case I was taken was waiting. They watched as I approached the dark glass behind which sat an immigration official who would check me through, or detain me. He looked at my passport and, unlike the National Guard when they stopped the bus to search my bags for guns, he checked my visa. He said something to me, but I, of course, could not understand and responded with my usual, "no hablo español." With that he picked up the phone and placed a call. Soon, a young woman in uniform appeared and it was obvious they were having a conversation about my visa and what they should do about it. They chatted for a couple minutes, occasionally looking toward me as if making plans for who should be called. If I ever wanted to understand the Spanish language, it was then, as I will forever be curious what the conversation between the two of them entailed.

When the conversation ended, I braced myself for the bad news. I was wishing I had remembered to pack my ruby slippers. Then the conversation ended. "Here it comes," I thought. The young woman turned to me, smiled, and walked away. The young officer told me the exit tax was six colons tax (equivalent of seventy-five cents), which I immediately produced. With that I was allowed to pass through security to my waiting plane to take me home to Iowa. I felt like a Christian who had been thrown into an arena full of lions, only to discover that they were all vegetarians. I escaped jail, or whatever consequences may have come of it, and thus ended my first life-changing trip to El Salvador. I knew I would return. I just did not know how soon.

Chapter 3

A Return Visit

> *"It is, hence, not happenstance or sentimentality, or even compassion that occasions the biblical association of God's people with the impoverished, the dispossessed, the imprisoned or the outcast; but that identification verifies and implements the confession that Jesus Christ is Lord."*
> William Stringfellow

In a matter of weeks after my return home from my twenty-nine-day life-changing trip to El Salvador, I was under care of a professional counselor for depression. I had gone to El Salvador to learn about poverty. So much more had happened to me than I could ever have anticipated. Beyond the darkness, at the bottom of that long, downward-leading stairway, from my thoughts and dreams, came forth the reality of the brutality of poverty that broke my heart, tying me to a common consciousness and spirit with my newfound Salvadoran friends. When I thought, from my limited view, what it meant, I found myself more confused than anything else. By faith, I embraced the truth that my life had changed and was changing. Sometimes life opens avenues to the unknown, and it is only time, and the fresh spirit of God's leading, that gives it meaning. This was, for me, one of those times.

My soul was engaged in a battle to center or realign itself. The trigger to the memory of a forgotten horror from my childhood was suffocation. When I heard Carmen tell about Vilma's suffocation, as they tried to hide from being found by the military, I was reminded of a time, long ago, when I believed I was about to drown by a man whose name I still cannot recall. He was a large man. I watched him lumber through the trees that separated the barnyard from the bare dirt of the front yard. He told me I could not come with him, but I was a curious child, and that curiosity took over as I watched him disappear into the area where we milked the cows. I walked to the other side of the barn, where there was another door I could peek through. I did not know what to call it at the time-- today we refer to it as bestiality--but, at the time, my young and innocent mind was filled with confusion and wonder. I was witnessing the reason for which he told me not to follow. I was discovered spying. His anger rose up like a frightening monster in my child's eyes when, out of the dark, he grabbed me and I was terrified by what he would do next. There was a horse tank filled with water for livestock nearby, and that is where I believed I was to die, to drown, as he plunged me into the water over and over again. My spirit was my means of escape. All that I recall was blackness enveloping my soul. Did I faint? Did my mind shut itself down from the viciousness being forced upon me? When I later awoke, I was on a pile of straw and knew then that something terrible had been done to me, something beyond the drowning. I had been violated in some way that my young mind could not quite grasp. I went to my secret hollow tree and cried.

The Presbytery of Des Moines has a strong social ministry root. It funded a large portion of CROSS Ministries, for which I had been founding director for several years then co-director with Sharon Baker for several more years. Through that ministry, and the founding of Hansen House of Hospitality, I was known for social ministry. In January, 1991, I presented to the Social Ministries Task Force of the Presbytery a proposal to make El Tablón an on-going mission of Presbytery. My advocacy for the homeless and those in prison had put me in the public light and there was a certain respect for what I said and did. I suspect for that reason, with minimal debate, the proposal was affirmed and recommended for the next Presbytery meeting docket.

The Presbytery meeting was held in March, 1991, at the Presbyterian Church in Allerton, Iowa. There, debate on the proposal raised several important questions and some respectful objections, but the placards of photos of the extreme poverty and hunger I had placed at the meeting set a compelling tone for a positive passage of the recommendation. I presented the information from the perspective of the Hunger Action Enabler for the Presbytery. The receptivity to such a relationship was enhanced by the fact that Cantón El Tablón was the recipient of half the Rural Harvest Offering that year. My sixteen-day visit to El Tablón prepared my mind and soul to speak from within the biblical mandate to feed the hungry. The vote was unanimous to establish the Sister Parish relationship.

People within and around Presbytery were somewhat astonished that the decision was made for a long-term commitment to El Tablón from the beginning. There is no clear perspective on why that happened without serious resistance. The Presbytery of Des Moines had a history of affirming God's call for preferential treatment of the poor. And the pictures along with the stories of poverty I recounted that day were a bit overwhelming. It appeared that it was truly the intention of God that the Des Moines Presbytery extends its hand of justice to El Salvadoran poor. It was simply meant to be. The desire to be in ministry in that country was emphasized that day with the vote to not only establish a mission relationship, but also that the El Tablón would receive half the offering on a yearly basis going forward. It was the first step that would grow Our Sister Parish Mission into an on-going mission in the life of Des Moines Presbytery. Nearly two decades after that momentous vote, Des Moines Presbytery can with pride claim Our Sister Parish Mission as a response to the Jesus' declaration *"to care for the least of these."* (Mt. 25.45). The scope of that mission can be found at www.oursisterparish.org.

It was in October of 1991 that I made a second visit to El Tablón. To the casual observer seeking a quantitative benefit of return on time and money expenditures, the trip was a foolish waste of resources. For me, such thoughts were outweighed by my promise to make good on my word that I would return for a second visit. I experienced a depth of appreciation that comes from just being present among those who struggle and feel forgotten. It became a reflective moment that affirmed my love for the Salvadoran people and fueled my own desire to participation in their struggle against the violence of their poverty.

My friend Don Fisher, a Presbyterian pastor, who was at the time serving as pastor in Lenox and Sharpsburg Parish of Des Moines Presbytery, suggested we go to Guatemala City to study Spanish for two weeks. The ability to speak the language seemed important, although the reality of how important it would be for my future had not yet been defined. So I accepted the invitation. While we were in Guatemala, I shared with Don stories about my trip to El Salvador, and the impact that the visit to El Tablón had made on my life. Since we were so close to El Salvador, Don suggested that we might make a weekend trip from Guatemala to visit the cantón.

After several days of negotiating with the Salvadoran Embassy for a visa, we were given permission to enter the country. It was official that we would be making the trip on the weekend of Saturday, October 19. Don and I were up at 5 a.m. to be at the airport by 6 a.m. for a short flight on COPA Airlines to El Salvador. I had contacted CRIPDES the day before to ask if people there could coordinate a day trip to El Tablón. I was pleased to hear that Lisa, whose last name my aging brain has forgotten, from CRIPDES, who did some of the translating for me on my first trip to El Salvador, agreed to be translator for Don and me. Francisco, who had business to tend in that area, was more than glad to drive us there. By 3 p.m. we had worked out all the logistics for the trip and were on the road to our yet-to-be-discovered encounter with destiny. I could not contain my excitement and the anticipation at this opportunity to revisit the friends I had made in El Tablón less than a year before, and the fact I was making good so soon on the promise I would return was also very gratifying.

For the second time in less than a year, I was on the Pan American Highway that winds its way through mountains toward the Honduran/Salvadoran border. We drove without much conversation on the winding, pothole-ravaged highway through and around pueblos. Poorly maintained centuries- old buildings gave evidence of mounting poverty, but it was the shacks nestled in the gullies and precariously perched on mountain ridges that expressed the poverty of that tiny nation, struggling with social and political uncertainties. The beauty of mountains and green foliage served as camouflage for the terrible poverty and devastation to human life that lay beneath.

We drove past sugar cane fields and banana trees that covered much of the valleys. They were large plantations that used large land areas for the export crops. Smaller fields of corn stalks from the year's harvest covered much of steep mountain terrain. I thought it was a great use of available land in the tiny country of six million people. The driver helped to put it all in perspective by explaining that the hillsides were the only land the poor could afford to rent in order to raise a crop that provided the daily tortillas for Salvadoran families. And even then there was not enough land for every family that wanted a piece of land on which to grow enough food for a family. The long civil war was still reaping a harvest of its own. The availability of land is essential in a place where there are so few daily jobs capable of paying a living wage, in an economy that lay in ruins following the war. President Reagan said it was a war fought against Communist aggression. Those are easy words coming from one who never knew true, grinding hunger in his life. They were words of political expediency that in no way imaginable spoke to the truth of why there was a revolution in El Salvador. For the poor, the FMLN battle against the wealthy ruling ARENA political party was to secure the right to health care, education, employment and, for the small farmer, a little piece of land on which to grow the daily plate of beans and tortillas.

We passed the beautiful San Vicente Mountain that I remembered well from my first trip. Banana trees were flapping in the breeze, women were carrying water in cantaros on their heads and oxen were pulling carts with their sundry loads, while groups of children played in the dirt in front of their adobe, makeshift huts that they called home. The hum of the Jeep motor and the passing of the landscape lulled me to sleep as I anticipated my soon-to-be-realized dream of returning to visit my friends in El Tablón.

I was jolted awake when the Jeep left the highway and surprised to discover that we had taken a different road than the one at Mercedes Urmana, which begins the ascent to Berlin six miles up the mountain. "A shortcut," the driver said, plus it would bypass the military checkpoint that frequently was set up on the road that leads to the cantóns on the mountainside on the other side of Berlin. Soon it became apparent that the shortcut was a poorly maintained stretch even by Salvadoran standards. We drove over and around boulders, traversed deep ruts and wash-out areas. Residents in the area, particularly children and barking dogs, began to appear along portions of the road to witness this amazing event of a car going by on a road where motorized vehicles were not a common sight.

The next thing I knew, Don and I were slammed against the front seats and the Jeep barked sharply to a stop. The left front tire had fallen into a sizable hole in the road. My gringo mind surveyed our situation and began to believe that the dream of visiting El Tablón was quickly evaporating. The only sign of life around us was the occasional footpath that left the road into underbrush and beyond, into what appeared to be nothing but a vegetation-filled unknown. Surely to find a tow truck to pull us out of the cavernous hole was hours away. The driver calmly surveyed the situation and then yelled something in Spanish as though yelling his consternation up to heaven. Within minutes, there were several men along with curious women and children coming from what seemed like nowhere from the underbrush. With a unified effort, several of the men lifted the Jeep out of the hole and sent us on our way.

It was well after dark when we arrived in the Cantón Las Delicias, a neighbor of El Tablón on the ridge across the valley. We went directly to the home of Julio and Angelita Munosis. Julio was the Directiva (the town council) president and in a brief conversation, Francisco had secured us assurance for food and shelter for our tired and hungry bodies. The house was missing an entire wall where a large oxen cart could be parked. There were at least six children of various ages who surveyed us with wide eyes that spoke of wonder about where we came from and why we came here. Animals wandered in and out of the house, including roosters, ducks, dogs, a couple of pigs, and a horse that never entered but stood vigil close by to keep an eye on the situation.

Francisco, along with Julio, left for a meeting right after a dinner of beans, rice, eggs, and tortillas. They woke me from my fitful sleep when they returned about midnight. I remember wondering what there was to do in the middle of nowhere so late, and in retrospect, I realize how ignorant I was about reality there. It does not take a rocket scientist to figure out that there are ongoing strategy meetings in time of war, and a war was going on. The next morning the evidence of war became visual as planes dropped bombs in the Berlin area that, as the crow flies, was about two miles away. The military operation that had been launched meant the probability that there would be checkpoints at various locations through which we would pass. The roads were slick from rain that had fallen in the night. That, in and of itself, was sufficient reason to walk but, with the military operation in full swing, we now had been provided the absolute reason not to drive. I soon learned that a routine walk to Salvadorans could be a strenuous effort for out-of-shape gringos. Single file, we disappeared through tangled vines and tall grass on the edge of the ridge that defined the cantón's perimeter, onto a path that led down into the valley below.

It was an hour and a half walk from Las Delicias to El Tablón. It was an easy trek as we made our way through a maze of fallen trees, boulders, and waterless ravines to the bottom. When we got to the bottom of the valley, we paused for a break for a moment before the demanding upward trek before us that led to the ridge of El Tablón. From that perch that overlooks the entire river valley is a view of Salvadoran terrain that is nothing less than indescribable heavenly beauty, but on looking inward toward the cantón and its activity, from its perimeter, it is a bleak reminder of a pathway to an indescribably difficult life.

As we climbed, I could see off to the right skeletal remains of a mansion that once had been the command center of the family that owned the entire land area. Families in the cantóns served as the labor force to harvest the sugar cane and cotton that they grew in the valley. The laborers were not paid in colones, the currency of El Salvador at the time (in the early 2000s the Arena government changed the currency from colones to U.S. dollars); the poverty wages they did receive were paid in script. Each plantation printed its own that was coded by color so merchants would know with whom they would exchange the script for colones. Script could only be used as exchange in the Berlin market. It was not possible to spend it outside the Berlin municipality. The burned remains of the mansion served as a vivid reminder of the justice issues, script payment being one of many that ignited a war that seemingly was never going to end. Seeing this scene grieved me and caused me to wonder how much destruction and how many lost lives it would take to bring the calm of peace and a sense of justice to the land of El Salvador.

We reached the ridge through the tall grass and brush that surround much of the cantón. I could hear voices and smelled the burning wood used to cook the pots of beans and tortillas. A home made of saplings set vertically, with mud that filled the gaps between them, came into view, and then the people doing their daily necessary tasks for survival appeared. Someone pointed at us and in unison, as though rehearsed for a play, all ten or twelve people present turned to see the intrusion into their lives. Someone smiled, another yelled, and we were greeted with the typical, genuine hospitality unique to the people living in poor cantóns. Vigorous handshakes and pats on the back gave indication of recognition and that I had returned as I had promised I would. People gathered around, and a young man ran off to spread the news that visitors had arrived. It was an affirmation to my spirit that confirmed that this was to be a place that would define my future.

Lisa, our translator, a young woman with long strawberry blond hair, told them our visit was to be brief, as Don and I had a plane to catch back to Guatemala that evening. They immediately confirmed it would need to be very brief as their "alert network" had informed the cantón that the Salvadoran military was advancing toward their homes and to expect them to arrive within an hour. They expected trouble and, although we were welcome, we had to leave when the military got closer.

A woman whose name I cannot recall who served on the Directiva of the cantón came toward me. Her eyes glistened with tears that I immediately learned were from gratitude she and others felt for my return to visit. She said that often my name was mentioned in conversation among them and they would wonder if I remembered them. My return, she said, was a note of encouragement that someone, somewhere knows they exist. I wondered if the people of El Tablón ever were recipients of good news as I listened to her tell me what had happened since my departure. A granddaughter had been kidnapped. She was two months old when it happened and although they think they know the one who did it, they did not have sufficient status or political pull for action to be taken against the man. A young girl of one of the families had been randomly shot by the military and the army has been particularly harassing the community, threatening to burn their crops for being supporters of the FMLN. The threat was somewhat hollow as the crop was predicted to be 20 percent because of severe drought.

It was a hurried chat we had, but in that short time I was reminded how quickly children there have to grow up. Walter, one of Carmen's sons with whom I had lived on my first visit the year before, had, since my visit, turned twelve years old. Twelve was the magic number that had been decided by cantón leaders. Twelve meant he was old enough to fight in the war. I watched him as he joined the other men but mostly boys in their teens to prepare for the battle that would inevitably happen. He checked his rifle to make certain it had ammunition before he secured it onto his shoulder with the strap. Our eyes met and he moved my way to say goodbye. In nearly a year since I had last seen the lad, he had grown more muscular and strong in stature. A prideful but bashful grin exposed his teeth and he said something to me I did not understand. I beckoned Lisa to come translate. He repeated his words again, which were, "I am a soldier now in the revolution. Please pray for it to end so our children can grow up in peace." They were powerful words that indicated a clarity over which the war was being fought. He was one of the first of many children I came to know, boys and girls, who never got to experience the joys of childhood and went from a little boy's world to a man's world and from a little girl's world to a woman's world. There is no in-between adolescence in the land of violent poverty. That is a First World luxury available to far too few children in the world today.

Word spread quickly that we were visiting. The usual hospitality of something to drink was brought for us as more people arrived to talk with the visiting gringos. Stories the women had told me on my first trip to the cantón flashed in my memory; military torture that created walking zombies, death squad night time hits that left families forever grieving and wondering what happened to their disappeared loved one. That same military was currently approaching our location. Questions permeated my solace. Where would those I loved be able to hide in safety? Would anyone die in the gun battle about to take place? How does the mind maintain sanity in the midst of the fear that permeates every part of their world? The price war exacts is enormous, but the hunger and social discord that is the root of civil war moves the human mind beyond that cost to hope for a just life. A life in which people can find room for life's basics needs and wants: food, jobs, and perhaps even education, and so much more that we of the First World wallow in at will. Within an hour, someone gave the alarm to leave and we ran off down the mountain we had ascended an hour before. A wave of nostalgia swept over me as we left the cantón. My heart again affirmed to me that the people we had just visited would define my future, and who I was becoming.

When we returned to the humble home where we had slept the night, the woman of the house had soup waiting. Although it was only 11:20 a.m., I felt hunger from the difficult walk we had just made to and from El Tablón. We consumed the lukewarm liquid quickly, aware of the drive back to the San Salvador airport in time for the plane's departure back to Guatemala. We quickly gathered our personal items and with hurried goodbyes and words of gratitude for the hospitality, we sped down the dirt road that led out of the cantón. So we ate and ran, but to no avail, for out innocent visit to El Tablón had made us, two Presbyterian ministers from Iowa, the "enemy" and thus subject to being detained. We were stopped no more than one hundred yards down the road by the military in front of the cantón's Catholic Church. The one in charge took our documents and left a handful of very young soldiers, surely no older that sixteen years old, to guard us with their U. S.-supplied M-16 rifles. My mind drifted back to the night of the commemoration march for the slain Jesuits and two women from the UCA I had participated in a year before. Weapons in moments of uncertainty are frightening and dangerous. Weapons in the hands of very young boys can have tragic consequences. For some reason beyond my understanding, I was not afraid at that moment. I was worried, however, about our being detained at the hands of Salvadoran military. We had a plane to catch.

I had been stopped by the military before. This time it was different. No one was asking questions of us. No one was going through the Jeep or trying to ascertain where we had been and where we were going. It was just the young Salvadoran military with their rifles at ready and us, waiting for word to proceed, or not. Time seemed to crawl on like a turtle on sand. Fifteen minutes passed and the translator wondered out loud what was taking so long. When a half hour had passed, she expressed concern that we could be in harm's way. The military had murdered people for less than this and who of us knew what was being currently discussed by the command. A sense of foreboding caused acid reflux from the soup I had hurriedly consumed. I looked directly into the eyes of the young soldiers holding us captive with M-16 rifles provided by my government and bought with my tax money. Anger stared back at me, and it was apparent that we were the enemy and they would relish the opportunity to put a bullet between our eyes.

The passing time led to pensive thoughts that this was not the sort of usual military stop. I wished for connection with the outside world that would give us a vehicle for negotiation with those in charge. Then I remembered. I had one such vehicle in my briefcase from Iowa Senator Tom Harkin's office. My friend of many years, Mike Messina, had campaigned for Sen. Harkin, and the idea of having a "letter of introduction" on the senator's letterhead came out of his concern for my safety in traveling to Central America. It was a simple letter of introduction, which stated that Sen. Harkin knew me from my childhood, when we lived in the same community of Dexter, Iowa, and that he asked I be given safe passage and treated with the care any traveling U.S. citizen should receive. It was the same year the senator was a dark horse candidate for president and his name was one that would be recognized in Latin America. I dug the letter out of my briefcase and asked the translator if it might help. She didn't know but felt it worth getting into the hands of the military officers. So she asked one of the young soldiers guarding us to take it to them.

He disappeared into the grass and bushes that lined the road. We waited in silence. It was a moment frozen in time. Another trip made without ruby slippers. Even the dogs were silent and the ever-present chickens had disappeared. Up to that moment, I couldn't remember a time of ever being envious of chickens. There was not a human being in sight save for the young Salvadoran soldiers guarding us. Suddenly, the isolation was broken by a soldier that appeared to say we could proceed to the next checkpoint. The young soldiers guarding us parted, as the Jeep engine revved and we jetted forward with the urgency we all felt to get as far away as possible. Only another one hundred yards or so forward we could see the next checkpoint. We stopped short and the translator and driver said they would go talk to the soldiers. They exited the Jeep and walked toward the soldiers. I watched the young woman with long strawberry blond hair gently tease them, talking with animation, and it was apparent her friendly conversation was part of a survival mode; a tactic I'm certain one learns soon when in the presence of uncertainty. I saw the heads of all at the checkpoint turn as from the tall grass and bushes along the road came a U.S. Air Force officer. At that time, U. S. Command allowed no more than fifty military advisors in the country on any given day, and this officer was one of them. He was a tall man with a grim look. I was thankful to see our passports in his hand. He handed them to the translator and talked with her briefly. When they returned to the Jeep, she said he told her to tell us to get the hell out of there and to never come back. The consequences of our visit might have ended differently another time.

On reflection, the whole incident brought to my mind a scene from the Book of Acts, in the twelfth chapter, when Peter was imprisoned, chained, and heavily guarded. An angel of the Lord appears and mystically delivers him from the prison cell and sets him free. Up until then, I had never had cause to think of an angel of the Lord appearing in the form of an U.S. Air Force officer, but, after all, they do wear wings.

It is difficult to evaluate the value of experience in the moment it happens. But in the months following, my inner reflections provided additional fuel for the fire of the spirit burning in my soul. The walk from Las Delicias to El Tablón reminded me of pain-filled lives of the people there, caused by the oppressive acts of the rich that take advantage of the poor. Words of the prophet rang in my ears. *"Let justice roll down like waters and righteousness like an ever flowing stream."* (Amos. 5.24) NRSV. If not here, then from where would justice roll down? The visit with my friends in El Tablón served to confirm my relationship with them and that it would be an on-going process to discern what it meant for my life. Certainly, all that Jesus taught that I had embraced was pushing me to act, though I could not yet imagine how to move forward. It was perhaps most disconcerting to discover the presence of the United States Air Force officer who returned the passports. In reality, the U.S. government contributed $1,000,000 to $2,000,000 a day to fight the war against the poor of El Salvador, and the officer was a personification of that ugly truth. Millions spent daily to fight a war that could have solved so many problems.

It was no longer a statistic on a page. It was a reality. It should give us all pause to consider that our tax dollars were helping to pay for the crucifixion of those who had captured my heart. I thought of Jesus on the cross, and the words that he proclaimed as his life was bleeding out of him, *"Father, forgive them, for they know not what they do."* But, in fact, we do know what we do, our government does know what it is doing, and it tallies it up to "collateral damage." Mention Communist invasion, and the U.S. government has a blank check to do as it pleases. And so my prayer for a calling became one of teaching people both inside and outside of the Christian community the truth of what we were doing to the poor of El Salvador. I was reminded of the response of the prophet Isaiah, when seeking an affirmation for God to his call, *"Here am I, send me!"* (Isa. 6.8).NRSV. And just as quickly, there came to me the response of the prophet Jeremiah's to his call from God, *"I cannot speak for you, I am but a child!"* (Jer. 1.6). Time would be the factor to give me clarity and to know for sure, not when, but how I would be called to speak the Word of the Lord in the land called *"The Savior."*

Addendum

I am deeply grateful to Rev. Don Fisher for his suggestion that we visit Cantón El Tablón. It was an important moment in my call that would become a new focus in my mission and life. And I want to offer my sincere apology to his wife Laurie for risking Don's neck. But it was, after all, his idea to go. Don is a Presbyterian pastor who at the time of our visit was pastor in the Des Moines Presbytery serving the Lenox-Sharpsburg parish. In 2004, Don and Laurie moved to Kansas City, Missouri, where Don took a call at the Second Presbyterian Church, where he continues to serve today as an associate pastor.

Chapter 4

No One Is an Island

"No man is an Island, entire of itself; every man is… a part of the main; any man's death diminishes me, because I am involved in Mankind; And therefore never send to know for whom the bell tolls; it tolls for thee."
John Donne, Meditation XVII

I have always affirmed to others that if the Holy Spirit lays something on your heart, you have to seek every means to somehow live it out. One has to embrace a turning away from the multitude of obstructions that can spring into your path, to knock you off course, and embrace the stature and authority to live, say, and do what you must in the next step of your walk of faith. To do less is cowardice. Worse it is a denial of discipleship with the Lord Jesus Christ. Little did I know that the moment for such a decision about a visit to El Tablón would soon be mine to make.

The frequent presentations I had made about my trip in November, 1990, to El Salvador became well known testimony to my growing interest of the people there, especially those who lived in El Tablón. So it was little surprise when I was invited to join a student delegation from Simpson College in Indianola, Iowa, on a trip to that land. Marilyn Mueller, a Simpson professor of management, who was to be part of the leadership, asked me to help educate the students about the country by telling the story about my own visit. The carrot for me was that El Tablón would be on the itinerary for them to visit.

It was January, 1992, near the time of the signing of the peace accords to end the twelve-year civil war. We had arrived at the Salvadoran airport early afternoon and had settled into one of the many bed and breakfast-style hotelitos available to travelers. It was at the orientation meeting I learned about a change in the schedule, that our agenda would not include a visit to El Tablón. The decision was made by on the ground leadership from a college in Minnesota. He was not familiar with El Tablón.

Before dinner we went to the CRIPDES office to meet with organizers who, among other things, helped those displaced by massacre and war violence, to organize. I had been to that office on my first trip in 1990 when I joined the repopulation caravan (see Chapter 2 - 16 days in El Tablón). We entered the office where a handful of the staff and some visiting Salvadorans were preparing to educate the Simpson College delegation. Among them was a curly haired man who looked familiar but I could not put a name to the face, let alone remember where I might have met him. As I considered whether to go introduce myself to see how I knew him he caught my eye. He smiled and came toward me with an outstretched hand, saying my name as he approached. The next thing I knew with the help of a translator I was in a conversation with a man who was from the El Tablón area.

El Tablón was in an FMLN controlled area; it had been an area of conflict throughout the war and he saw no point in the visit. It was obvious that any argument I would make about the merits of the trip were futile and, with some consternation, I resigned to the fact it was off the schedule. Before dinner we went to the CRIPDES office to meet with organizers who, among other things, helped those displaced by massacre and war violence, to organize. I had been to that office on my first trip in 1990 when I joined the repopulation caravan (see Chapter 2--Sixteen Days in El Tablón). We entered the office, where a handful of the staff and some visiting Salvadorans were preparing to educate the Simpson College delegation.

In our chat I learned he did not live in El Tablón but in the neighboring cantón of Santa Cruz. But he visited El Tablón often. He expressed thankfulness that the military stop, which Don Fisher and I had experienced the year before (Chapter 3), had not turned tragic. He also said that many were grateful for the return visit I had made. That confirmed even more that, even though the college representative had nixed the visit for the delegation, I would do everything in my power to make the trip myself. So I explained my dilemma, that I had come with a delegation and the visit to El Tablón had been eliminated from the itinerary and I would be most grateful if he knew of any way I might find someone to help me go there. I was overwhelmed with gratitude by his response. "I am going home tomorrow! It's on the way, and I can take you there if you want." "If I want," I shouted in my mind. Going there was the magnet that made me part of the delegation in the first place. He said he would pick me up the following morning at the hotel where we were staying. Now all I had to do was to tell the rest of the delegation.

I did that at dinner. The delegation leader from a college in Minnesota was sitting across from me. I had rehearsed over and over how I would tell him and the rest of the delegation that I was going by myself to go El Tablón the next day. Finally, in what seemed the right moment, I told them the news. He listened as I explained how it had come about, the importance El Tablón had taken in my spiritual life and not going there would be the worst thing that could happen to me on the trip. To his credit, he did not protest but simply said he hoped I had a good trip and wished me the best. He ended with, "I want you to know that I am not responsible for anything that could go wrong by your leaving the group to go on your own." I thought to myself, "What can go wrong? I know the way."

As planned, my friend from Cantón Santa Cruz picked me up early the next morning in an old Jeep that was missing one door. I knew "a way" to El Tablón, and I learned that there is more than one way to get to there. As soon as we began the trip, I was lost.

Though we had left early in the morning, it was nearly 3 p.m. when my guide let me off at the entrance to El Tablón. Carmen's house was my destination, which was about a half-hour walk. I felt the anticipation one feels when going home and no one knows you are coming. However, the secret I thought I had was not well kept, and it was not the last time that, without radio or telephone, a group would know I was on the way even before I got there. Their human communication network is incredible and, of course, one of the main resources they have for survival and protection from unwanted visitors. When I arrived, there was a group of at least fifteen people waiting under the large tree in front of Carmen's to greet me with open arms.

News of my arrival brought a revolving door of visitors. I was without a translator but it didn't seem to matter much. The time I had spent at the language school in Guatemala the year before had given me some basics of the language. But, it would be only when I moved to the Casa Pastoral in Berlin, nine years later, that I would gain an element of fluency. Included with the visitors were some of the revolutionaries who stayed for dinner. Then, the same three women who had made the hundreds of tortillas as I met on my first visit (chapter 2) arrived and the eggs were cooked and tortillas grilled. Then, there came another familiar face. His name was Jesús. He was always sort of in the background, or would arrive late at night during my first visit. He slept on a cot in the back of Carmen's house and was always gone when I got up in the morning. I sensed a fierce protective spirit behind the gentle and mild-mannered presence he had. For the first time he approached me to greet me and give me a welcome.

There were about twenty people in all when the strum of a guitar broke through the night air alit by a bonfire that another had prepared. I could smell the aroma of hot, sweet coffee just before someone placed a cup of it in my hands quickly followed by a plate of beans and eggs. Carmen had learned from my first visit that my favorite fruit was bananas, a man placed an entire stock of the tree ripened fruit next to my chair with a signal of his hand that they were mine to eat. It was time for Radio Vinceremos broadcast of war news from the perspective of Santiago, a man from Venezuela who come during the war and decided to stay. By his efforts the alternative radio station was established to broadcast the FMLN view of the war, which was a constant thorn in the side of the military. An old battery powered radio was set on the dirt and everyone listened intently with every word of war news broadcast by Santiago.

Though I could not understand what was reported, I could tell from the couple cheers and few hand claps during the broadcast that the news was good.

Radio Vinceremos is a legend in El Salvador's annals about the civil war. Santiago and his radio broadcasting crew were the single most important source of news from the FMLN revolutionary perspective. By necessity, they had become adept at broadcasting on the run in order to escape the intense efforts by the military command to search him out and destroy the broadcast, in particular, Colonel Domingo Monterrosa.[11]

The guitar music resumed after the radio broadcast. I knew from experience that the party could go late and by 11 p.m. I found the bed I had used on my first trip in 1990 ready for me. I drifted off to sleep, fully aware that rats in the rafters above my head would be accompanying me for a night's rest. They were not exactly part of the family but not as intrusive as they had seemed on my first visit. Apparently, I had been accepted into their family, and we were familiar comfort to each other. I slept.

I woke about 3 a.m. to silence and a very gas-filled and painful stomach. I had diarrhea, and the bathroom was still the open field behind the house. I found the dead-bolted door in the dark and groped my way out of the home and onto the open moonlit field that still served as the

---

11   Monterrosa was commander of the Third Infantry Brigade was perhaps the most feared and most hated general in the Salvadoran military. He was infamous for his training in massacre operations at the School of the Americas when it was located in Panama and before being moved to Fort Benning, Georgia. Soon after his training, Monterrosa was assigned to become the leader of the elite and controversial Atlacatl Batttalion that was known for massacre tactics and ruthless murders. It is rumored that Monterrosa was present and directed most of the thousand massacres that took place during the 1980s. The legend goes that out of vengeful retaliation for the pain and suffering he caused In 1984 the FMLN revolutionaries booby-trapped a fake rebel radio transmitter that was then left in a field by the radio broadcast crew that apparently had been caught off guard by the approaching Salvadoran military. Monterrosa took with him the radio base as his trophy onto a helicopter to fly back to San Salvador. The bomb went off while he was in flight, an attack planned by Joaquin Villalobos. The remnants of his helicopter can be found in the Museum of the Revolution in Perquinn, Morazan departmentt. El Salvador officially still honors him as a military hero. (Source: Wikipedia)

latrine. After three trips within a half hour, there was no doubt I had a serious case. With resignation to my unplanned problem, I lay down on a grassy spot nearby and saved myself from those numerous trips I would have made.

By 5:30 a.m. there was stirring in the cantón. Carmen brought me water and I was thinking the concern that no one uttered out loud was dehydration caused by severe diarrhea. Without intervention, death is certain. The water was passing through my body as quickly as I drank it, and I was rapidly becoming dehydrated. It was a six-mile walk up the mountain to the bus in Berlin that would take us to San Salvador. I felt a sense of desperation, but knew there was no alternative and so with the morning light, we started walking.

Julio was chosen to be my companion for the return trip. A number of children and dogs and a few adults walked with us to the edge of the cantón. From there a chorus of voices sent us on our way with the familiar que le via bien. We cut through the trees on the path that led to the steep short cut that would reduce the distance to Berlin by a mile. The lack of medicine and transportation became life and death matters.

As we neared the incline that would take us out of sight of the cantón, I turned for one last view of the place that had claimed a piece of my soul. God willing, it would become not just a place, but a piece of my destiny. The group that had accompanied us was still where we had left them. I knew they did so with troubled hearts, watching as one does a friend who is leaving until he or she is out of sight, as though to claim a piece of one you might never see again. Rehydration was futile. I drank water and within minutes, it passed. Sparing the reader morbid detail, I can tell you that the same aggravating and uncomfortable problem in the states becomes nearly overwhelming and disabling in Third World countries. I saw death knocking at the door. I remembered the words the guide for the Simpson College group had said on my departure, that he would not be responsible if anything went wrong. This was a great lesson in Third World travel, if I lived to tell about it.

I was weak and dizzy to the point of having to stop often just to gain some energy to move on. My head ached. For the first time in my life, I thought it was likely I would die. Not just a possibility, but likely. And even if dying was not a reality, it felt like a good option, rather than going through what I was feeling at the time. I clearly understood why immigrants from Latin America, in their attempts to cross the Arizona desert, just cannot go on and get left behind just because there are not resources to do any differently. I knew I was not going to be left behind, but I also knew there sometimes is just nothing anyone can do.

On reflection, I know I would not have made it home if my friends had not decided on a plan of a man with a horse. Julio led me to a house on the path, and there was a horse ready for me to ride. I hate horses. Even more, I am afraid of horses. But this time it did not matter and I gladly allowed the men to lift me onto the horse's back to give my rubbery legs relief. I am not sure for which I was most grateful, the horse to carry me the rest of the trek or the tall pine trees that rise above the parish of St. Joseph church bell tower in Berlin when they came into view. Within fifteen minutes after that sighting, we were at the bus and shortly after we arrived the engine of the two-decades-old Bluebird bus revved, and the blast of the horn signaled this bus was leaving.

Julio and I sat in the back seat and the blare of rock music from the speaker just above our heads compounded the headache I already had. I was grateful that Julio was with me. The experience was illustrative of the importance of having companionship in uncertain and painful times. It gave new meaning to the timeworn phrase, "No person is an island." Previously, I had thought of that phrase as meaning to have power to affect group change. I did not think of it as the absolute means of survival. Julio was talking with a young woman dressed in white in the seat next to us. She was a nurse at a nearby clinic so he gave her his seat so she could examine me. She looked at my eyes and my hands. She pinched the skin on my arm and a ridge remained. She looked concerned and then talked with Julio some more. A few minutes later she said three words. "Hospital in San Vicente." I said, "No."

It was a long drive to San Salvador with frequent stops to allow people to board and to take on more people. Some carried with them chickens and sacks of grain destined for the market. Women with the traditional apron secured around their waist came aboard with baskets of fruit and vegetables to sell. At one point of the journey, the aisle was jammed with standing room only. The windows were open but even then the aroma of chickens and humans packed into close quarters made the air stuffy, which just made my headache worse. If I had not been so sick, it might have been an interesting study in Salvadoran culture and transportation. But I was sick, and at that moment had had my fill of culture and its difficulties, the difficulties these people live with all the time.

When we arrived at the bus terminal, Julio brought a cab to the bus because the cabstand was too far away for him to carry me. He gave the driver the CRIPDES address and while I could not understand the Spanish language exchange of words between Julio and the driver, I did know Julio had told him to hurry.

Medical people were waiting when we arrived. They carried me to a bed in the clinic and immediately hooked me up to intravenous bottles of liquid. Then I slept. It was late in the evening when I awoke to find Josie, my translator from the first trip, sitting by my bed. She smiled and took my hand to give me assurance that now everything was OK. Then she scolded me. She affirmed my continued attempt to relate to the poor of El Salvador, but that I needed to remember that it is not a *one-person* effort.

I arrived at the hotel where the rest of the delegation was staying in time for breakfast. I related my adventure to them, and when I finished, Marilyn suggested to the university guide that if I could get to El Tablón by myself that surely it would be OK for the delegation to make the trip to see El Tablón of which I was always talking. He somewhat reluctantly changed the schedule and they went there the very next day. I still felt weak for such a distance to travel, so I stayed at the hotel. I was a bit jealous, but inwardly satisfied, that the delegation would be able to see and come to know the people of the cantón who had grown to inhabit so large a place in my heart. Mission accomplished.

Chapter 5

Out Of The Shadows

"It costs so much to be a fully human that there are very few who have the enlightenment, or the courage, to pay the price.... One has to abandon altogether the search for security, and reach out to the risk of living with both arms. One has to embrace the world like a lover, and yet demand no easy return of love. One has to accept pain as a condition of existence. One has to court doubt and darkness as the cost of knowing. One needs a will stubborn in conflict, but apt always to the total acceptance of every consequence of living and dying."
Morris West, <u>The Shoes of the Fisherman</u>

By early 1993 the Cantón El Tablón was a household word among my acquaintances. Three times I had visited, and the ongoing poverty, the violence of the war, the social discord, and political shenanigans I had witnessed or learned about in El Salvador made that piece of my life a private nook of meditative reflection, walking with God in the garden, like fellow travelers, passing though a mysterious and emotion-laden territory. In that walk I felt a renewal of spirit, having left behind the depression of those early El Salvador days. But still I lacked clarity in my mind to envision where the walk might lead. All I knew was that my experiences of traveling to and through that land had opened the eyes of my soul, and they were changing the way I lived. They were the birth pangs of a new life.

Poverty defined the social fabric of more than half of El Salvador's six million people. The repressive political dictatorships that ruled the nation for decades were tools of U.S. foreign policy used to control its interests in El Salvador and other Central American Third World countries. In return for the river of money flowing from the U.S. into those nations, we held title to their souls and their future. And the use of death squads was also seen as acceptable and necessary tools for use by the U.S. State Department in order to politically dominate the poor and repress the oppressed voices that screamed out for justice. It was a legitimized means of domination and control that was good for business or, what some on Wall Street might refer to as "business as usual."

Historically, it began back as far as 1932 with this stark and horrifying example. During that year, coffee prices bottomed out and the plantation owners who were our coffee suppliers were mistreating their workers, paying them very low wages and forcing them to work in appalling conditions. The poor, mostly indigenous men, were led by a fellow worker named Farabundo Marti in an organized and united refusal to cut (harvest) coffee that year. The government came to the aid of the plantation owners by sending troops into the western part of the country where the discontent was brewing. Over a three-day period, the troops massacred an estimated thirty thousand people.

That stream of government-sanctioned violence, as a means of solving inconvenient problems, has never stopped flowing, like a river of the blood of martyrs, up to and including the more recent killings of the four American religious women, Monsignor Oscar Romero, six Jesuit professors at the University of Central America, as well as the mother and daughter who kept their house and cooked for them. These are illustrations of the extent to which the Salvadoran government and military were willing to go keep the control, keep the wealthy happy, and keep money flowing from the north with the stamp of approval of American foreign policy and commerce. Tens of thousands of Salvadoran poor and human and social rights advocates, who spoke up for justice and reform, have been brutally murdered over many years by the military and sanctioned death squads in the name of some bizarre form of budding democracy that could only have been spawned in concert with the privileged and elite who had a buck to make on it.

In the face of the experiences I had directly with people who had suffered this repression, I began to question my own non-violent theology. Such a theology did not seem to have legs to stand on in view of the aggressive violence constantly perpetrated against the poor. A nice and neat Catholic or evangelical theology, shoveled like manure in North and South America, often encourages the poor to focus on the rewards of an afterlife, which rings out to me of simply being yet another form of the repression. The liberation theology that I had studied over twenty years earlier when in seminary suddenly took on a renewed definition that began to make all the sense in the world. There was no doubt that the revolutionary Army (FMLN) had grown out of the teachings of liberation theology. They were also branded as communists for their opposition to the so-called "democratically-elected" government of El Salvador. The wealthy class was constantly bothered by the threat of a civil war led by the FMLN revolutionaries, who were committed to fight for social and political rights of the poor.

My theology and social analysis were being reshaped by what I was witnessing, and my critique of U.S. foreign aid policy became something of a fly in the ointment when I talked with church groups and individuals about U.S. actions and how their tax dollars bankrolled the repression of the Salvadoran poor. I argued that the individualism we enjoy is a First World luxury and that U.S. foreign policy had wrongly labeled the revolution in El Salvador as a communist threat.

True, it was a threat to the democracy that the U.S. was prompting in the region; but that was because the U.S. foreign policy was not promoting the kind of democracy we enjoy, but rather one that would keep one particular party always in control in El Salvador, one that appeared to be freely elected. So one could say that it was actually a form of communism that the U.S. was supporting in El Salvador in the name of American democracy; a communism that favors the wealthy and powerful in that nation. It struck me that it costs the world a lot for the U.S. to be free.

I began to advocate revolution in that it was, in fact, a necessary act of defense and an instrument necessary to achieve social and political gains for the poor. I began to include the theory of it in my talks to churches or individuals who wanted to hear my story. It should not come as a surprise that my talks were not always well received and, in fact, I was often told that I was endorsing communism. In addition, friends and family, who have their own lives and concerns to live with, came to consider that what had consumed my spirit was no more than a peculiar curiosity to them. Any telling of it was akin to TV news with thirty-second sound bites to express what was on my heart. Beyond that the eyes glazing over and discussion often turned into an argument about what our responsibilities are to foreign nations, and that there is plenty of poverty right here in the U.S. for me to be concerned about. Of course, they neglected to recognize that I had already been engaged with the poor of Des Moines for a number of years and they had not.

The truth can hurt too much when it clashes with patriotism or national pride. So I was frequently reminded to realize there are tragedies just as significant here in the United States to be addressed, though they could never quite formulate anything so tragic as a thirty thousand-person massacre. And always there was the defense that maybe the U.S. did donate lots of money to the government and army of El Salvador, but how certain was I that communism would not get a foothold in our hemisphere if we hadn't. The discussions I did have developed into political and social diatribe rather than participating in a discussion about the life of struggle of Salvadorans. As a result of these differences of approach and understanding, the desire to ground my spirit began to focus inward and I came to depend more on prayer and my own lifestyle analysis.

I made subtle and some not so subtle changes in my life. Perhaps the most public and obvious was that I began to ride a bicycle for transportation. I rode it in winter and summer, rain and shine, and used a car only when I had to drive more than twenty-five miles out of the city. In doing so, without deep analysis about what it meant, in a symbolic way, I set myself apart from the world of abundance that claimed First World comforts at the expense of two-thirds of the rest of the world. Since I did not have a car, my friends were extraordinarily patient with me, when I arrived to borrow theirs. My anger flared at the proliferation of coffee shops where people paid up to four dollars for a cup of special brew when I knew families that struggled for their lives, having picked that coffee for two or three dollars a day. The struggle to define the disparities I experienced was turning me into a loner in the crowd. I began to talk less about my personal struggle, to thwart the subtle suggestion by friends and family that I had been there and done that and had forgotten I have a life. Jesus' injunction, *"Take up your cross and follow me,"* took on a new understanding in my life. Life went on, but the train of life left me at the station without a map indicating where I should go next, or a schedule as to when the next train would arrive. And the cross I was carrying was becoming a bit heavier each day.

I can look back now and think to myself, what else did I expect? Patriotism, and the prevalent belief that we as a nation are God's own chosen people, lead to the notion that we deserve all our comforts that come at the expense of the poor in developing nations. And the truth was, I too, benefited in my comfortable male, Caucasian, First World life, all of which made my protest a little tricky. However, I knew that my personal experiences and avid reading had taught me over two years that my life was not the same, nor would it ever return to how it was before I made that first trip to El Salvador in 1990. I could not ignore the stirrings it caused in my soul if my faith was to mean anything to me and stand for anything at all.

My frustration with making myself heard was beginning to turn me further toward the darkness of cynicism. The Desert Storm U.S. invasion of Iraq lit up TV screens like it was the latest run of a movie, and the half-truths in the news that victory brought freedom were reminders to me of the violence the poor were suffering in El Salvador. No doubt it was as true in Iraq as well.

The darkness began to envelop my being, not unlike that which I had experienced during my first trip years earlier, in November, 1990. But the darkness did not lead to depression as it had the first time. Rather, it became to seem like a "think tank," with me inside seeking ways to make sense of this newfound faith walk. It was my good friend Frank Cordaro who brought light into the surrounding darkness. He suggested it was my aloneness in the issue that was my problem and that if others in the Presbyterian Church were to become of like mind regarding El Salvador, then I might have to leave the valley of darkness I was becoming increasingly comfortable in and experience living in the light again. He was right, of course. I needed to provide to others the experience I had lived so they could join me in this new journey that was taking shape. Light had to shine into the darkness of widespread ignorance of what was really happening in El Salvador. I now had the knowledge to open a way to shine that light. It was yet another reminder to me that no person is an island, that I needed others with me in this mission; and that the alternative was to migrate toward becoming nothing more than an angry, useless voice in the wilderness, railing against the poverty created by greed, violence, and control. Others over the centuries have done just that, and it hasn't worked out too well for them over time. I wanted to be wiser.

Seeing is more than hearing, and smelling is more than seeing and hearing; and observed poverty touches the heart more than just hearing about it. When you add the inevitable putrid smell, it creates a lasting impression. An "official delegation of the church" made sense, and within a couple weeks I had traveled to many Presbyterian churches within Des Moines Presbytery to find willing people to make the trip to El Tablón. A few from other denominations heard about the trip and called to inquire. Within a couple months there were eighteen people signed on to go to El Salvador and, in 1993, the first official Presbytery delegation made the journey. As the time grew near for the trip, we met as a group to review the planned schedule and talk about the trip. In that meeting I knew the struggle had turned into new energy, a renewing spirit, a hope generating in my soul. I knew then that I would no longer be a lone voice in that struggle.

I remember few specifics about the trip itself. We went to the usual massacre sites in San Salvador to lift up the personalities of the Jesuit professors and two women, Monsignor Romero and the four American women, all martyred because of their love for the people and their advocacy for basic rights of the poor. The civil war had ended a year earlier, in February, 1992. But there was still an occasional military stop, although it was less intense with even a friendly exchange. But the poverty remained.

Members of an early Presbytery Delegation

Children at play on a dirt floor, threatening U.S. Democracy.

The "picture window" view of the landscape from elevated seats of the chartered bus that had been our transportation for the week provided clear looking of the Salvadoran mountainous and lush green landscape. As of yet the delegation had not been up close to the country's poor, they had not yet had conversations with them that would, as it had for me, sear a corner of their hearts with sadness. We were on that bus, headed to the Cantón El Tablón, the place of my own personal experience two and a half years earlier, where members of the delegation would receive their initiation into the truth about poverty, real Third World, poverty.

There is something almost idyllic about the shacks that dot the mountainside that would be perfect for an artist's creation. The stench of poverty is hidden beneath that mountainous beauty and green foliage. Women who carry colorful cantaros filled with water can be imagined as a choreographed dance of Latina beauty. The fifty pounds that the cantaros weigh when filled with water is an invisible factor. It becomes an emotionless scene where you only see beauty, but you do not know the woman's name, or her story, or her burdens. Groups of children playing do not communicate the infected sores or other tragic health problems they suffer with limited hope of medical care available. I trusted that the truth of poverty, long hidden by the beauty of the people and the land, would seep into the hearts of the delegation participants when they came to know even one of these remarkable people by name and hear his or her story. Soon they would relate directly with those in El Tablón, and there they would "suffer" the same truth that wounded my soul. You cannot relate directly with one who suffers and not feel the pain of it. When you know them as people and not as foreigners, it affects you at the very core of your being.

The group had a translator for community meetings to hear what the residents of El Tablón had to tell. They told of the war and the lives it claimed. El Tablón, we learned, was essentially a repopulation community of people who had fled their homes of many years in the face of advancing troops of the Salvadoran Army's scorched-earth strategy, destroying every living being and everything that could possibly lend support to the FMLN force. They had fled from one of the hundreds of massacres the Salvadoran Army committed in a strategy called 'taking the water away from the fish." They killed entire communities of men, women, and children, old and young, to eliminate any possible support for the FMLN revolutionaries. Then they told of the massacre at La Quesera, not more than five miles from where we were that took place on October 23-24, 1981. Over two days, six hundred and seventeen men, women and children were slaughtered by the Atlacatl, Atonal and Pipil Salvadoran Army battalions.

Words were not needed for the visiting gringos to see the lack of adequate nutrition and medical care. Watching the children, some with swollen bellies, or a festering cut added urgency to the need and right for families to have access to land to grow food crops. That right had been included in the peace accords signed to end the civil war, but the process to obtain the land was slow and frustrating. But they knew it would happen and you could see the hope that, in short time, life would be better and their children would have full stomachs from the fruits of their labors on their own piece of land.

In the meantime, there were expressions of simple wants. The school for elementary children in El Tablón was being reopened soon. The Des Moines Presbytery had sent a grant of $8,000 to repair the roof and clean out the tons of dirt that had washed into the building over the years it had been closed due to the dangers of the war. They needed school supplies so their children could study, such as notebooks, pencils, crayons, and all the things we take for granted in First World schools. Another obvious and often requested need was clothing for their children, some of whom were seen playing nearby in tattered dresses and pants. A few could be seen with nothing more than underclothing.

Two delegation participants, Rev James Rae and Joyce Bassler, who since then has become an ordained Presbyterian pastor, hoped to help with the need for clothing. That was the first inkling of a dream turning into reality, the realization of hope for solidarity with a mission. They began to talk about organizing a clothing drive. They would collect clothing and send it by freight truck from the U.S. to the cantón. The need was so overwhelming, and soon the logistics of organizing such an effort began to sink in. And the oft-spoken truth that it is better to teach a person to fish than to give a fish, was being incarnated at that very moment in the midst of these people from such different origins and background. Ideas were springing up all over. Maybe they could collect money to teach a handful of women in the cantón to learn how to sew. Maybe then they could make their own clothing as the need presented itself. Maybe they could even eventually sell the clothing or other items back in Iowa. All the way along the trip home from El Salvador to Des Moines, the delegation members were planning their strategy for raising the money to start the mission. A major sewing project in El Tablón was born.

Presbyterian Women organizations of Des Moines Presbytery were contacted and asked to donate money for the cause. The women's groups stepped up to that plate and became the source of funding for the project. In mid-1994, a little more than $2,000 was put in the hands of Padre Protasio who was the head priest at the Parish of Saint Joseph in Berlin. A sewing class began for six women from the cantón. Five times a week for six months, the chosen women would walk the six miles up the mountain and learn the techniques of sewing. Then they would walk back down the mountain to their homes to resume their difficult lives of hauling water, gathering wood, cooking for the men, and doing all else to create some semblance of life in the presence of unspeakable poverty. For those six months, they held in their hearts that the sewing skills they were learning would give them and the families of the cantón something that was not possible ever before. Hope rose in the eyes of the people as they pondered one more way their lives were changing for the better. It was by faith they believed the next piece of what they needed to complete the project would come: sewing machines.

Projects that come out of a quest for justice and are driven by faith have a way of moving forward as quickly as questions are posed. People in the churches in Iowa knew sewing machines were needed. So what if the women learned how to sew? How would they sew? Mike McHugh, then director of Catholic Peace Ministries in Des Moines, heard about the education the women in the cantón received and began a campaign to collect treadle sewing machines to answer the question. He was helping to organize donations for a Pastors For Peace Caravan that would be passing through El Salvador in the fall of 1994, and the machines could be hauled by that caravan. People throughout Iowa donated treadle machines that had been stored in attics and sheds, machines that had been replaced by more modern electric machines. In all, ten machines were donated and by the time the women had completed their sewing course, the machines were deposited in their homes for production of clothing for the children of the cantón. In January, 1995, fabric that had been purchased with donations from the Presbyterian Women of Des Moines Presbytery was used to sew skirts, pants, blouses, and shirts for the sixty-six children from the cantón that would be attending school that year. Mothers stood proudly with their children dressed in the clothing and gave thanks for the many people who had made that possible.

When the official Presbytery delegation members returned from their trip, I sensed solidarity of common hope to bring a semblance of justice to the people on the mountainside of Berlin. The sewing project became the first "hands on" effort, and a personal knowledge of the poverty moved a core group forward with a call to work for peace and justice in El Salvador. The word of El Salvador ministry spread among several churches and suddenly I no longer felt alone in a ministry, but now with a growing number that would ultimately create Our Sister Parish Ministry on the mountainside of Berlin. Obviously, a sewing project would not change the social structure that brought repression, but it instilled a hope that change could come.

Since that delegation fourteen years ago, there have been literally hundreds of people from many different faiths visit Berlin and the seventeen cantons on the mountainside. The entire shared experience of the creation of a sewing co-op, and the varieties of people of faith who contributed to make it possible, rang through the hills and mountains of the area the truth of the biblical sentiment, faith the size of a mustard seed can truly move mountains.

Chapter 6

Rooting the Mustard Seed

I shall be telling this with a sigh Somewhere ages and ages hence: Two roads diverged in a wood, and I— I took the one less traveled by, And that has made all the difference.
Robert Frost

Jesus spoke to his followers, "The Realm of Heaven is like a mustard seed, sowed in a field; smaller than all other seeds. But when it grows, it is greater than other herbs, becoming a tree, so large that the birds of the air come and perch in its branches."
Matthew 13:31–32

His name is Protasio. His long, lanky legs give him a height beyond most Salvadorans, but his dark skin and facial features cannot defy his indigenous Mayan roots. It was late July, 1993, and I had come for a meeting with Protasio, the priest at the Parish of St. Joseph in Berlin, along with his assistant Friar Elias, health promoter Virginia Morataya, and Milagro Rodriguez, who was pastoral team organizer for social programs. The meeting was at their invitation sent through Mike Hoffman, the SHARE Foundation organizer for the San Salvador office. The invitation had suggested that they wanted to discuss the "good mission" that was happening in El Tablón.

Protasio was well versed in church history and explained to the others the Reformation roots of my Presbyterian faith. Conversation focused on my professional life and responsibilities it entailed. They were more than a little curious as to how, as a Presbyterian pastor, I had come to focus so much attention on the Cantón El Tablón. The four of them knew that I had visited El Tablón several times and that the last one three months prior was with a delegation of eighteen people. They were grateful for the statement of solidarity suggested by my consistent and frequent visits. However, they were concerned that I had focused my support and vision of solidarity on that one cantón. The liberation theology focus of the parish expresses a mandate of justice for the masses, and they felt that if I was to continue my journey within their parish, it had to be with all the people, not just those of El Tablón. It was their hope that I would agree to live at the parish for an agreed upon period of time to learn about the poverty in all the seventeen cantónes on the mountainside that made up the municipality of Berlin. What better way to do that than to live among them, to know their faces and their names, to hear their dreams, to know their pains, to experience their poverty lifestyle, beyond what could be learned in a short visit with a delegation.

The frequent smiles suggested friendship, but their eyes communicated a concern. Each trip, whether by me alone or with a group, included donations of clothing, shoes, medicines, and money for the community. Basically, the concern was that if I continued to bring aid to the few without solidarity for the masses, it would create an unhealthy dependence and, in the end, failure. No one person by himself/herself can be a vehicle of solidarity. Likewise, no one person (or one cantón among several) that receives aid can become the tree of justice that liberation theology promotes; especially when there are no resources of development for the masses when the gringos leave to go back to their comfortable existence.

They had not said I could never visit El Tablón again, but the implications of doing so were clear. The focus of my visits had to be the parish--all seventeen cantónes, with El Tablón but one of the many. It was another decision to be made, another step in the walk God began with me nearly three years earlier on the first visit in 1990. My heart felt heavy. While wanting to follow what seemed to be a continuation of that walk, the question of how to move to another country for a length of time became like a boulder in my path. I looked at the young woman who had come with me to translate the conversation. She said, "I understand your dilemma. Don't close any doors yet. Pray about it."

"I will let you know in a couple weeks," I told the four. They nodded their approval and expressed hope that I understood their wish, which was that I come live with them for long enough to get to know them and their culture. We said our goodbyes and then as we prepared to leave to catch the bus to San Salvador, Protasio quipped, "There is one more thing: you don't have to worry about tornados here. We have earthquakes, but never tornados nor hurricanes." Then he smiled broadly and with a firm handshake said, "We will be waiting for your decision. We hope you can find a way to come live with us."

My Salvadoran journey had reached a fork, and my future loomed in the truth of Robert Frost's poem, "The Road Not Taken." The team at the parish in Berlin had not forbidden me to visit El Tablón, but the implications of doing so without immersion with the people's lives and to experience liberation theology of the Parish of St. Joseph's had been made clear. To reject their invitation and continue my visits to El Tablón would make me an ugly American and, in the end, my visits would do nothing but foster dependency that ultimately leaves the community worse off than before. To reject their invitation and end my Salvadoran walk was to deny my search for meaning since my first visit in 1990, when in a house in El Tablón, my spirit was set free from brutality long denied. I was now free to sing a new song for the Lord, a song of liberty of those who are oppressed, a song of unity with the brutalized poor of El Salvador. Even in my freedom, accepting their generous invitation seemed to be nothing less than an impossible dream.

I had three options, and one decision to make. Clearly the first option would be to continue my visits without the immersion offered by the parish team. That was unacceptable in my mind so, it immediately became two options and one decision.

On July 1, 1975, I accepted a call from Cottage Grove Presbyterian Church in Des Moines as founder of CROSS (Christians Reaching Out Seeking to Serve) Ministries, an urban ministry that was a partnership between Cottage Grove and the Des Moines Presbytery. Rev. Dave

Reeves was senior pastor of the church, and it was his vision for ministry to the poor of the inner city that was the genesis of that ministry. I am grateful for his faith in my abilities to make that dream a reality. By 1980, Sharon Baker had become co-director of the ministry with responsibilities in legislative advocacy and direct assistance to the homeless and hungry. I did community organizing around homeless, hunger, and prison issues. I also served as Hunger Action Enabler for Des Moines Presbytery and as associate pastor at Cottage Grove. In the mid-1980s, my friend, Rev. Dave Madsen, became senior pastor. It was now 1993 and I was approaching a fork in my journey's road. One fork in that road was sort of an "Isaiah call," *"Here am I, send me."* (Isaiah 6.8). It was simply a leap of faith to continue the Salvadoran walk that had consumed so much of my spirit. The other fork in the journey was to remain at CROSS Ministries and live according to a "Micah call" *"... to do justice, love kindness and walk humbly with God."* (Micah 6:8). The struggle was between a future I didn't fully know or comprehend and a form of ministry that had served me well for eighteen years.

There was no comfort level for the making of this decision. The options at hand consumed my every waking moment. My flight home was the day after the meeting with the parish team, and as I walked down the ramp to the door of the plane, I thought of a saying a seminary acquaintance had crocheted and framed. "Theory without practice ain't shit." I began to consider that the invitation to live at the parish was my opportunity to practice the theory of liberation theology. But it would take more than a saying from my past to put me over the hurdle these decisions represented.

Two weeks passed and August came. The boulder in my path for deciding my future was as ominous as ever. Professional, family, and financial considerations lay over my mind like frost that covers the fields in harvest in October. I prayed and waited. The first crack in the boulder came at the CROSS Committee meeting in August. A change in my professional life would be the first, yet easiest decision. The agenda for the meeting included the usual: treasurer's report, direct assistant report, legislative advocacy agenda, Hansen House report (a hospitality house for men coming out of prison that I founded April 16, 1980, and Doug Maben expanded into Criminal Justice Ministries in 1984),

Homeless Coalition report and, last, a request to co-sponsor a March for the Homeless that would be held that month in preparation for the cold winter that was approaching. The sponsorship cost was $50. It was a routine request that we'd accepted without fail on many occasions. When a vote was taken, the request failed to win support. To my astonishment, my ears heard the answer to the request, "No." Someone stated, "Maybe we should not be spending our money on events such as this when there are so many people in need of food and shelter." At first I was somewhat shocked. I understood the rationale of the request to use it for direct assistance, but it felt a bit disingenuous at the same time. Direct assistance to the needy without prophetic witness fell short of my understanding of CROSS's mission and ministry. It was one of those incidents in life that cause us to choose "the path less travelled by..." And you know how the rest of the story goes.

It is important for me to explain that to friends and loved ones that my potential decision to live for a year at the Parish of St. Joseph in Berlin was radical and senseless. "You are going to do what? What will that mean for your future? Why would you do that? Think of how old you are." These and other questions expressing surprise and criticism became like a litany in responses to my decision to leave a highly successful ministry among the impoverished in Iowa in order to walk among the impoverished in a wilderness unknown.

I was private about my decision, until I announced my resignation from Cottage Grove. I entered into a time of feeling alone as I had early on after my first trip to visit El Tablón. But this time it was actually more, for after making my decision public, I not only felt alone, but also felt I had to defend my decision of leaving the mainstream of life for an unknown future. As I reflect now, it was a critique of many that I was betraying my call in ministry, and they just could not comprehend that the call of God transcends frontiers and cultures when justice issues are at stake. But the judgment was strongest from the political critique of a few. I heard more than once about our fight against communism in that region, and I should be careful about such matters, as though I was joining forces with the enemy.

It took me a year to make the preparations necessary to make the move to Berlin, where I lived from August, 1994, to July, 1995. It was that year's experience that became the watershed for what would become Our Sister Parish Mission in the municipality of Berlin in the mountains of eastern El Salvador some seven years later.

The aloneness of my decision did not continue for long. In September, 1993, I left Cottage Grove to become interim pastor at United Presbyterian Church in Newton, Iowa, for nine months as I made preparations to move to Berlin. I received calls of encouragement from several friends. Cooperative efforts began to develop, the most significant being the collection of treadle sewing machines that would be sent by Pastors for Peace Caravan that would be passing through El Salvador. The sewing machines were destined for El Tablón as part of the sewing project that had emerged out of the experience of the first "official" delegation in the spring of 1993. (see chapter V). Ranks expanded, and the aloneness dissolved into a walk of hope that was depending on the mystery of faith to keep us on track.

One person from Newton and two from nearby Colfax were my wellspring of encouragement and spiritual nourishment as I made preparations to leave the country to live in El Salvador. They would continue to be major support for development of Our Sister Parish Mission in the early 2000s. Those people are Rev. Bill Calhoun, pastor at First Presbyterian Church in Newton and Rev. Duane (Doc) and Sheryll Skidmore. Doc, after I met him, accepted God's call to ministry and became a licensed pastor in the United Methodist Church.

Bill's church was located directly across the street from United Presbyterian Church, where I served as interim pastor. At Bill's suggestion, we had coffee every Wednesday at a local restaurant. Bill was a great supporter of my decision to live in El Salvador for a year, and in our conversation he suggested that maybe First Presbyterian Church could form a delegation to visit Berlin when I was there. In the spring of 1995, a delegation from First Presbyterian did visit Berlin, and it was in a meeting with Milagro Rodriquez that a great lesson in the dynamics of forming relationships between the north and south was given. It should be noted that Milagro had served on the parish team since the signing of the Peace Accords in 1992. She is an intelligent, capable and charming woman with a commanding presence. In a meeting that included Milagro, a member of the parish team, and with whom I have worked many years. Bill had asked of Milagro what they could do, at Newton First Presbyterian Church, to help the community. Oddly, Milagro did not respond to the question. It was as though she did not hear it. So Bill repeated the question, and Milagro again was silent in response. So, Bill asked a third time the question about what to do to help, and she finally responded, "You can get to know us. And in the process, we will get to know you. You will learn to love us, and we will learn to love you. Then together we can decide if there is something you can do to help us." It was a classic and important response that only she, from her culture, could have offered. For it moves any "help" gringos can give out of the realm of their generosity (read: the "ugly American") that fosters dependence, into one of genuine love and care given within community of faith.

Before the week was over, Milagro suggested that a medical team would be valuable to provide medical exams to the poor in the cantónes. Bill organized the first medical team delegation the following year, and it became an annual event that continues as of 2011. In 2000 the Sacred Heart Parish in Newton joined the delegation effort. Veronica Mangrich and her husband Lee and her brother Tony from Cedar Rapids have become the major leadership to organize the delegations. In 2011 there were 35 doctors, dentists, nurses and volunteers who provided a wide range of medical services. Since that initial delegation in 1997, the efforts have provided thousands upon thousands of medical exams for the poor and brought thousands upon thousands of dollars worth of medicines for them, as well.

My other support came from Duane Skidmore, known as Doc by his close friends and his wife Sheryll from Colfax. I met him at a lunch counter in Newton in that year of preparation. When he sat down beside me, I had a Spanish language book open, trying to learn the basics of the language. He inquired if I was a student at the local community college extension of Des Moines Area Community College. I said no, I was trying to learn the language for when I moved to El Salvador in August. We struck up a conversation about the adventure I was facing, and as we prepared to part, he asked what I needed at the parish in Berlin. It was a time when email was very new, and I did not even know how to use a computer anyway. Out of concern for communication,

I mentioned a fax machine would be nice to have. About two weeks later I received a call from Doc. He said he had "checked me out" and found me to be honest and sincere. So he and Sheryll had decided to purchase the fax machine I needed. He asked me to meet him at the local office machine sales store at noon. When I arrived, he said he had researched the machines and had decided on the best option for me to have. It was a $1,200 plain paper multi-purpose machine. I did not see Doc again until 1997, when I was at a United Methodist orientation for new pastors. For three years before my decision to make a permanent move to Berlin, I served Gatchel United Methodist Church in Des Moines. We both were in that orientation to begin United Methodist ministry. We renewed our acquaintance that developed into a very close friendship. To this day, I consider Doc and Sheryll to be people I am honored to call my friends; and Bill Calhoun, as one who understands the true meaning of the vow we shared in our ordination, "Will you be a friend to your colleagues in ministry, and will you serve the people with energy, intelligence, imagination, and love?"

In the development of Our Sister Parish Mission from 2001 until my retirement, Doc and Sheryll provided me a car each time I visited Iowa to promote the mission. In 2003 I drove their car a total of 5,000 miles as I promoted the mission in Iowa, Missouri, and Wisconsin. It was their generous hearts and willingness to loan me a car (a new Volkswagen Jetta, beginning in 2005) that made transportation for my visits to Iowa possible.

I left Iowa in 1994, with no clear understanding how life would proceed; there was no way I could have ever dreamed of the successes that would grow over the next two decades into the mission that came to be and is now known as Our Sister Parish Mission. It has impacted hundreds, perhaps thousands, of lives in Central Iowa. And the benefit on the mountainside of Berlin in the eastern mountains of El Salvador is that hope has risen in the eyes of the people. Nine churches have sister relationships with cantónes on the mountainside of Berlin. Each church sends a delegation at least once a year to its sister cantón. In meetings with leadership and the community, decisions are made about the cantón's needs, and armed with that information their sister church determines the level of commitment they can financially support. St.

Catherine Catholic Parish takes a Drake University student delegation each year to learn about El Salvador, its politics, religion, and social reality. St. Catherine Parish has also developed a sister relationship with the Cantón Canacaste, in the western part of the country, that developed out of the tragic death of Reyna Sandoval, who died when I hit her with my car (See Chapter 7, "My Long Dark Night of the Soul"). The University of Iowa Wesley Foundation, led by Rev. Marsha Acord, takes a student delegation to Berlin each year and has adopted a young man named Erick to pay his university costs to earn a degree in psychology. Seven potable water projects have been built on the mountainside; two churches, a school, and sewing center have been constructed in cantónes. Thousands of dollars worth of fertilizer have been bought and distributed to poor farmers on the mountainside. Don Justo Coffee, Blanca's Bags, and Just Light Candles are economic development projects that have had various degrees of success, with the coffee bringing a monthly income to help with projects of the mission. One other project that has met with success was the development of a natural medicines project that continues to this day at the parish church, but is no longer part of the Our Sister Parish Mission. By July, 1995, when I went home to Iowa, I felt secure that a permanent walk had been established between Berlin, El Salvador, and the Presbytery of Des Moines. The extent to which it would affect my life was still unknown in the landscape of my future.

A University of Iowa Delegation

More than a decade later, in 2006, the vision of mission had grown beyond the scope of my administrative abilities. So in August of 2006, I made the difficult decision to retire. I can hardly believe at times how seeds can take root and grow in seemingly impossible conditions. The events recorded within this chapter speak of that mystery, and of how the mustard seed of faith grows to become a bush greater than any other giving home to all the birds of the air. And, it most certainly can be said, it has only just begun.

Chapter 7

Blood Soaked Soil

> *"A voice is heard in Ramah, lamentation and weeping, Rachel cries out for her children and refuses to be consoled, because her children are no more."*
> *Jeremiah 31.15 NRSV*

A memorial wall in Cuscatlan Park in San Salvador records the names of the civilians murdered and missing during El Salvador's civil war. No one has an exact number, but there is agreement that there were at least 75,000 persons of all ages killed in massacres and abducted for murder by death squads. The exact number of massacres is unknown, but the parish team with whom I worked in mission said there were more than 1,000 of them throughout the land. In the time I have lived in El Salvador, I have had the opportunity to talk with many people who escaped a massacre or had loved ones killed in one. Some of those people are from Berlin, and their families lived in La Quesera, which is on the mountainside of Berlin. The massacre site I remember most is the first one I visited in 1994. It was in El Mozote. This is my story of that visit.

El Mozote is a cantón in the northeast region of El Salvador in the state of Morazan. My visit that day in the fall of 1994 brought anguish to my heart and soul.

The crackle of gravel beneath my feet brought memories flooding over me of my visit to the concentration camp in Auschwitz, Germany, several years ago. The same eerie silence I sensed in that camp punctuated the sound of my footsteps as I walked through the central plaza of the cantón. Ghosts of violent deaths flooded into the recesses of my mind. It took little imagination to hear echoing screams of terrorized children. Rufina Amaya, the lone survivor of the El Mozote massacre, the site of which I was visiting that day, had told reporters in an interview that she heard her own children crying out for her.*"Help us, Mama, they're killing us. Help us, Mama!,"* she heard her children cry over and over from her entrapment in a large house on the other side of the central plaza from where soldiers held the children. There were two hundred and twelve of them, as well as a few adults crammed into the small church rectory. First those children and adults were shot through the door and windows, and through the side of the simple house.

Then the Salvadoran army unit burned the house down to ensure everyone in the house was dead. A small monument near the church marks the location of the rectory where these most innocent, some as young as one year, were slaughtered.

Rufina Amaya with Bob

After Vietnam, U.S. Foreign Policy makers conceived of a strategy they dubbed "low intensity conflict." In places like El Salvador, death squads were trained at the School of the Americas at Fort Benning, Georgia, to implement the strategy designed to frighten the citizens of the country into submission. In El Salvador, if the wrong ears heard you speak of the right to land, education, or health care, death squads mysteriously arrived in the night and the tortured and murdered body of the "guilty one" would be found the next morning. Fear was the method of governance and control.

This massacre in El Mozote was one of the thousands mentioned earlier in this book as part of the low intensity conflict designed to cause fear among the people, referred to also as the strategy of "taking water away from the fish." The fewer the people willing to help the FMLN, the weaker they would become. The FMLN Revolutionaries fought mostly in the country until their offensive in San Salvador, the capital, in 1989, proved they were an army to contend with; and not, as U.S. and Salvadoran officials desperately were trying to get people to believe, simply a band of drug-running delinquents. People in the cantónes were seen as support for the revolutionaries and thus regularly targeted for sanctioned abuse. The strategy was to remove the support to the FMLN provided by the rural and mountain people by terrorizing, torturing, and killing the residents in cantónes that were from heavily populated FMLN areas. By doing so, the theory was that support for the revolution would be eliminated and the war would soon be over.

The massacre at El Mozote took place December 8 and 9, 1981. As mentioned above, in pursuit of this twisted policy, more than a thousand other massacres took place throughout the country. The war lasted another eleven years following the El Mozote massacre. So much for the strategy of low intensity conflict and the theory of taking the water away from the fish.

The first thing I saw, as I drove the long dusty road to the center of the cantón, was a large memorial on the far side of the central plaza memorializing the 1,000 Salvadorans murdered in El Mozote. A stone marker in the center of a small garden reads, *"They have not died. They are with us, with you, and with all mankind. El Mozote, December 11, 1981."* Most of the deaths were women and children, although a good number of men were also victims. A large tree stands guard over the monument that provides shade in the heat of the day.

It is a well documented massacre that the U.S. Embassy, in the days following would not confirm, even though photos of decomposed dead bodies along with livestock, dogs, and chickens had been obtained by two reporters from two major U.S. publications within two weeks of it happening. Confirmation of such violence would be a blow to the newly elected Reagan presidency, and so the embassy stonewalled the truth of what it knew. What the embassy refused to confirm has been detailed in the book, "The Massacre at El Mozote" by Mark Danner, one of those reporters who visited the site and documented the massacre.

El Mozote lies to the east of the main highway going north from San Francisco Gotera to Perquín. Mt. Colorado rises on the Salvadoran/Honduras border to form part of the majestic mountain range that separates the two countries. Knowledge of a military operation was known days in advance and many families from the El Mozote area fled over those mountains when they heard about it. Others believed the word of a well-known evangelical in El Mozote that he had the military commander's promise that people in that cantón would be safe from military harm. Many who did not flee to Honduras went to El Mozote, believing the official fabrication that it would be a sanctuary for anyone who chose not to flee. It was a lie concocted by the Salvadoran military and, likely, the U.S. military advisors, who were present on the day of the massacre. That is the reason there were so many people in the cantón when the massacre happened. They all shared the same false sense of security. Surely no one would dare do something so public and so horrific to non-combative people. I believe it was C.S. Lewis who once wrote that the greatest deception that Satan can tempt us into believing is that he doesn't exist.

Today "guilt money" has assisted with construction of homes, businesses, a remodeled church, and a community plaza as well as two wells drilled in the center of the cantón. But the day I visited in 1994, it was more of a ghost town, with few residents and one general store where essentials for living could be bought. A row of bombed out homes with bullet pock marks provides a corridor to a large home two blocks from the central plaza where women were led to the slaughter. The open fields served as an arena in which the soldiers raped, tortured and dismembered the younger women before they were routinely murdered on site. And the wall of the cantón's church was the backdrop where men were lined up for the firing squad.

I sat on a park bench in front of the monument that lists names the of victim's families. Twenty yards away, beyond the gate that leads to the church, is the monument to the children. My heart ached, and my mind grasped for anything that could help me to understand how people become capable of such horror. Nothing came. I sought to understand how human minds, people with families, neighbors, and friends become so hammered into hardness and viciousness that would permit the human soul to rape, plunder, and murder, as if it was all in a day's work. Nothing came to me, and I felt so very empty. I prayed forgiveness for my homeland that was complicit in this shame. I was not to judge, but wondered how it could be given. And if that were true, how could I attain some sense of forgiveness for myself, for, I thought, are not we all part of the same land, thriving off the fruits of all its wars?

I sat on the park bench for I don't know how long. I thought about my own children, now grown men, and the pain it would cause me for them to die before me, let alone hear their cries of fear and torture in the torment of massacre. As I looked across the central plaza, I could find not a single sign of life. Not a person, not a bird, not a dog. Nothing moved. Nobody was in sight. I thought about Rufina Amaya, that lone survivor who was found a week after the massacre near the river below. She had been the last living person of that fateful two days. How lonely, how sad, how mad she must have become.

My aloneness brought a shiver as I tried to imagine Rufina's desperate attempt to survive those days alone, having helplessly witnessed the murders of her children, for whom she could provide no comfort.

Children's Memorial at El Mozote

I didn't want to be alone anymore. I stood with the intention of going to the store across the central plaza. As I did, I caught a glimpse of movement out of the corner of my eye. I turned to look and saw two children standing about twenty yards away. I don't know how long they had been there, but it was obvious they were curious about me. They giggled at each other as they made their way closer. Their youthful innocence lifted my consternation about the massacre as a cloud of fog disappeared with the morning sun. They made their intentions known immediately. "Darnos un conlón?" I gave them each a conlón they asked for and asked their ages as I did. They were nine and ten, too young to have experienced the massacre. But one of them pointed to one of the names on the monument and I understood enough to know the family she referred to was her aunt and cousins.

My Spanish verbal skills were limited, but conversations can happen with children without a lot of spoken words. Their family had moved to El Mozote four years before. They had moved into their aunt's home. They had heard the story about the massacre from their elders and indicated for me to know more, I should follow them. First we went to the children's monument next to the church. Then they each took me by the hand and we walked across the central plaza down the dirt road between the houses with bullet-pocked fronts, around the corner to where a house once stood, the same house where young mothers had been brought to die, the same house with their corpses which had been burned to the ground. It had been excavated by a forensic team from a country in South America, as had been the rectory. The bones of the massacred had been buried at the memorial in front of which I had been sitting when the children arrived. They led me to the mounds of dirt where the excavation occurred and where the house once stood. They began to dig, making their own excavation with their hands.

Torrential rains and natural elements had leveled the mounds of dirt that had been piled high as the excavators looked for bones of the victims. The girls poked and dug, glancing toward me with serious expressions as if to say this is important and that they had done it before. I sat on the ground and watched them, until one of them stepped back and said something, then knelt down again to bring forth what she had found. It was a tiny bone, a perfectly formed, but very small human bone, the bone of an unborn fetus. Along with the women who had been murdered were the fetuses of who knows how many pregnant women. *"Hay muchos huesos pequiños dejado,"* or there are a lot of little bones left, the children said.

Evidence of the massacre remains in the blood soaked soil of El Mozote. They kept digging and kept brining me evidence of the massacre. There were bone fragments, bullet casings and pieces of clothing. I left them to dig and walked back to the pickup. My mind and heart were closer than ever that day to the reality of pain and death that filled the land of El Salvador during the civil war of 1980 to 1992.

When The Sun Comes Up in the West

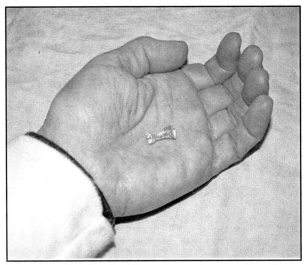

Picture of actual infant fetal bone from El Mozote burial mound.
Photo courtesy of Carolyn and Dan Rogers

I took the "evidence" with me to Iowa on one of my return trips to promote Our Sister Parish Mission. I so much wanted to use them in my presentations for promotion of the mission. I thought it might bring people closer to the truth of the brutality that El Salvador had suffered in the war we helped create and pay for. But they never quite fit into the theme of my talks. They are appropriate for these memoirs in photos that are included in this chapter. I have had them packed away for sixteen years and brought them out of hiding to emphasize the question that should be on everyone's mind. How did the United States of America, the land that dearly fought for its freedom from oppression find its way into this violence against the innocent?

In all the times I have visited El Mozote, twenty at least, the eerie silence of death and tragedy fills my soul and I never visit that I don't visit the excavation and think about all the little fetuses that were part of the massacre many years ago. There are lessons left in the blood soaked soil of the massacre of El Mozote. Perhaps as the next generation grows and the renewal of the cantón continues, the spirit of life will return, and the blood will become fertilizer for a new chapter of life and living for the people of El Mozote. Until then, I encourage all visitors I take there to remember that which is written on the memorial in "El Mozote... nunca más... never" again.

Rufina Amaya with daughter and grandchildren.

Chapter 8

Dark Night of My Soul

*For in this sepulcher of dark death the soul must needs abide,
until the spiritual resurrection for which it yearns.*
St. John of the Cross

Huge tears streamed down her cheeks to form nickel-size mud circles between her bare feet. She stood two feet from me and her red eyes, swollen nearly shut from crying, told the story of her grief. I had been given the best chair, a well-worn red plastic one that is common in the cantónes of the Salvadoran countryside. They are cheap but utilitarian to provide a seat for visitors to the humble homes of adobe and dirt floor. Sisters and brothers, aunts and uncles, mother, and this little girl with red eyes from crying gathered around me. A policeman with hand on his pistol stood on the fringe, eyeing the crowd around me for any sign of anger or vengeance that could induce violence. Alejandro Lopez, my friend, my bus driver for delegations, my son in El Salvador, stood by him vigilant for my safety. Within minutes, the kind expressions in words and actions of family members had set the tone and the two of them retreated a short distance to the barbed wire fence that separated the property from that of the neighbor.

The little girl's name is Reyna, named after her mother with the same name. I searched the crowd of faces for Cristian, her brother, who Reyna, the mother, was dragging with her as she ran in front of my car the afternoon before to cross the busy highway to a waiting pickup that would haul her and Cristian home. He was not there. My heart leapt to my throat. Was he dead, too? It seemed an eternity, though it had been just the day before at 5 p.m., when the image of mother and son appeared just yards in front of my 1997 maroon Honda Accord. I was traveling sixty miles per hour on the busy Pan American Highway. My friend, Kent Newman from Des Moines, whom I had gone to Guatemala to bring to San Salvador, screamed, "Look out!" and in the same moment, the car slammed into Reyna's running figure. At the moment of impact, I saw the fear of her eyes that met mine, then the weight of her body smashed the windshield and she fell onto the pavement. It became one of those slow, terrifying moments that seem to go on forever as my car careened onto the shoulder of the Pan American Highway at kilometer 34. I jumped from the car, hoping the woman would get up and walk. I saw blood from her head trickle toward the side of the road, and I instantly knew she was dead. Dead. I don't believe there ever has been a worse moment in my life. I scanned the crowd that had gathered and saw the boy, Cristian, dazed but alive in the care of a young woman. Traffic slowed and like a caravan chosen to live the next chapter of tragedy, and sadness flowed in the faces of cars that slowed to pass by death on the highway.

The clock on my cell phone read 2 p.m. It had been just twenty-one hours earlier and Cristian was alive at the time of the accident. I asked no one in particular, "Where is Cristian?" He was sleeping, and would be OK, but suffered some facial trauma from running into the side of the car, as he was a step behind his mother as she dragged him behind her. I recognized Reyna's mother, whom I had met the night before, and her brother, who had been the spokesperson for the family. They came forward and the policeman and Alejandro moved toward us. The mother bent to hug me as I sat in the chair and then suggested we go inside the home to complete the business for which I had come. I rose to follow her, with Reyna's brother, the policeman, and Alejandro following. Reyna's brother moved a door into the opening and placed a large plank to secure it. Then we began to count out five piles of one hundred dollar bills until it equaled $5,000 cash we had agreed on the night before as payment for Reyna's death. With the transaction complete, the brother asked if I wanted to view Reyna's body. I did not. I excused myself and went to the car in front of the house. I called

Kathy Mahler of the Compañeros, and told her that in that moment that I did not care if I died.

Within minutes of the accident, on the preceding night, the Transit Police had arrived. They took the keys to my car and then set up traffic barrier to divert traffic into one lane of the highway, around the lifeless body that was scrunched like a pretzel face down. I called Daniela, mother of one of the several families I have unofficially adopted in El Salvador. She told me to flee the scene. I told her, "No," without mentioning the police had the keys to the car. Before the night was over, I came to understand the reason she told me to flee. Her first concern was that the family would do me harm. Fear often motivates those who hit a person on the highway to leave the scene immediately. In addition, the law is that the driver pays the victim's family an amount that is negotiated immediately, and the driver of the accident, no matter whose fault, goes to jail for seventy-two hours. It is the law. It is El Salvador's way of insuring everyone involved will show up in court. There are no lawsuits in this country. The matter is settled immediately.

The two policemen were efficient. Within minutes, a pickup load of Reyna's family arrived to load her body into the pickup bed to carry her to the hospital. Two of the women in the family came to talk with me. I did not understand their words, but their expressions were kind. But even so, I noted one of the policemen immediately appeared by my side when they approached me. They left with the body and the rest of the family and I sat on the side of the road to ponder the death I had caused; what one always fears and hopes never happens. The tow truck came for my car. The sun set in the west as a steady stream of Sunday traffic slowed to survey what had been the scene of tragedy. The blood that remained and the presence of the police left no doubt that tragedy had struck at kilometer 34.

Daniela arrived with her friend and she helped me begin the process of calling those I needed to let know what happened. We began with the insurance company. She spoke briefly and then ended the call. She said, "They will send an attorney to meet us at the hospital where they took Reyna's body."

"Why?" I inquired. "Why tonight?"

"To negotiate how much you will pay the family for her death."

"But, it wasn't my fault," I stated emphatically.

"It doesn't matter," she replied. "It is the law. I told you to flee." Soon, I was to learn yet a new lesson of my life in this adopted homeland.

The policeman came to tell us Reyna had been pronounced dead on arrival. I was not surprised by his news. Then he said, "You are under arrest." By that I was surprised, and looked at Daniela for an explanation. Daniela said, "It is the law. You will go to jail tonight for seventy-two hours." At the end of the night Daniela was surprised and I was grateful for the kindness that was shown by the policeman investigating the accident, in spite of the law.

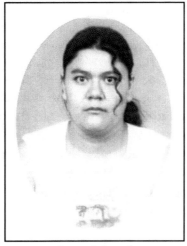

Reyna Marisol

The police finished their report and told me to get in the back of their car. I asked if I could ride with Daniela, her friend, and Kent and he reminded me I was under arrest and, no, I could not. There were no door handles to exit the back seat where I rode. And there was a screened barrier between the police in the front seat and me. I truly began to feel like a criminal. He drove with red lights flashing as though we were on our way to an accident instead to talk about money and how much I would pay for the daughter, sister, wife, mother I had just killed with my car. The lights of Santa Tecla, the suburb of San Salvador that had been my destination, came into view on the mountainside. I yearned for home, my own bed at Daniela's hospitality house in San Salvador, and to be able to go back in time before this terrible tragedy occurred.

As we approached the long, steady climb to the city, we made a left turn onto a poorly lit gravel road. It was a bumpy ride a couple hundred yards before the public hospital that served the poor of the region came into view. A tall security fence surrounded the facility and the large gate to enter was securely closed. Behind that fence I could see the eyes of at least a dozen people carefully scrutinize the police car I was riding in come to a stop a short distance from the fence. I knew those gathered to be Reyna's family. The policemen approached the fence and, after a brief conversation, returned to tell me the family was willing to wait for the attorney that my insurance company was sending to negotiate the amount the family would be paid.

The policeman opened the door of the car and invited me to stretch my legs. At the scene of the accident, he had asked me what had happened and he had written it in his report as I told the story. I had nearly cried as I told him the story. He asked me how I was feeling and suggested witnesses had confirmed that there was nothing I could have done to prevent the accident. The conversation turned to why I was in El Salvador and the work I did with the parish team in Berlin. His official demeanor of policeman turned soft and engaging as he listened to my story and how I came to be a missionary for the Presbyterian Church in a country where there is no Presbyterian Church. When the lights of a car came into view, he asked me to return to the back seat of the police car and, once again, I was reminded I was under arrest for a crime I could not possibly have prevented from happening.

The car was that of the attorney for the insurance company. He came to me and, without telling me his name, he said he was my attorney and that I had a policy that would cover $3,000 of the payment to the family. If they held out for more, I would have to pay the difference. I explained to the attorney that I was not a wealthy person even though I am from the U. S., and that I had no more than $1,000 in my bank account. He nodded and walked away to the fence to begin negotiations. Having been a pastor for so many years, it felt so different from my numerous experiences with families and the loss of loved ones. It felt so strange to be putting a price on death.

I considered giving them the $4,000 I had available if they asked for less than that. I could not hear the voices but my intuition told me the attorney's hand movements indicated bad news. He returned to the car and asked if I could raise $7,000. They were asking for $10,000. It was then I learned that it would be best to reach an agreement that night, as I was required to go to court in a few days and there it would be asked by the judge if all parties had reached an agreement for closure of the case. If not, the court would likely mandate for me to pay what the family asked, within reason. My being a gringo, it was likely a judge would render a judgment that was close to the family's asking. If I refused, I could be sent to prison. There was a certain irony to it all in that I had spent a great deal of my vocation trying to get people out of prison and now I could face being in one.

I sent him back with the news I had $4000, three from my insurance company and an additional one thousand dollars of my own and, I reiterated that I am not a rich man. It was time to plead for mercy. It was time to tell the world what happened, and to ask for help. Kathy Mahler's phone number was the only one I could remember as a member of Compañeros, the group in Des Moines that oversaw delegation schedules that visited Berlin to support Our Sister Parish Mission. They also were the fundraisers for the mission. I dialed it on my cell phone and waited as it rang four times. On the fifth ring, I heard, "Hello."

"I killed a woman with my car. I need help." Even as I said the words I was in a state of wondering who it was speaking into the phone. Was that my voice? There was a long moment of silence. The message was more than words. Fear and sadness fell like noise of hail on tin roofs. Finally I was able to explain to Kathy what had happened. I had an accident, a woman was dead, it was not my fault, but I had to pay according to the law, and was there any money Compañeros had in the bank she could access for help in the negotiations that the family had begun at $10,000. She said she would call me back and hung up the phone.

I told the attorney I had called the states to ask for financial help. He told the family. Then the Salvadoran wait began. It is a cultural thing where time becomes irrelevant. When factors of the unknown became part of the equation, like waiting for a phone call for information, then time stands still. It will happen when it happens. The policeman invited me to stretch my legs again. The half moon that had been high in the sky began to fall behind the San Salvador Mountain. I felt trapped like an animal, preparing myself to be killed by the predator that had been seeking me out. I felt deeply, fearfully alone.

Daniela, her friend, and Kent had gone for something to eat, the attorney was passing time in conversation with the policeman and the family was huddled together to stem the chill of the evening that was getting late. Headlights of a large vehicle filled the pothole-filled road and a huge double cab pickup pulled up to the gate. I had been ushered back into the police car and when I could read the sign on the pickup door, I understood why. The office of the attorney general had been called to talk with the policemen about the accident and how the state would proceed with the matter. The gate opened for the pickup to enter and two men exited from the cab that had made them appear much larger than they actually were. I was surprised that one was no more than five feet tall. The two men, along with the two policemen, called to Reyna's brother and mother and the six of them entered a garage attached to the hospital where Reyna's body was waiting to be taken home for burial preparations. Fifteen minutes later the representatives of the attorney general drove away and left us to wait for Kathy's phone call and for the coroner to come.

Kathy's call came. She was sorry it took so long but she could not reach many of those on Compañeros, but those she talked to said for sure there was $1,000 available and they would do whatever necessary to get more, if needed. I passed the information to the attorney, and then asked if I could talk with the family. After conferring with the police he said yes, that they did not feel there was any animosity toward me. I approached the fence and began by saying, "May I please talk with you instead of using an attorney to negotiate?" They were happy to have the conversation. At first we did not talk about money. We talked about Reyna. I asked her age. She was twenty-two. I asked if she had children. She had two, Reyna, six years old and Cristian, four years old. I asked where they lived. They live in an adobe hut next to her husband's parents, but he had gone off to Mexico a year before and they did not know how to contact him.

One of the sisters asked where I was from. I told them I had two sons in Iowa, but that I had worked with the Equipo Pastoral (pastoral team) in Berlin for the past five years. I told them I truly did not have much money, but with the call from Kathy I could guarantee them $5,000. The older brother who had been negotiating with the attorney said they had hoped to get enough to construct a cement block home for the children, maybe with water and electricity. Their negotiating had not been out of greed, but out of love for the two children who were orphaned living in dirt. He said that $5,000 was more than enough for the funeral, and he asked if they could talk about it for a bit. I retreated to the car and waited that Salvadoran wait.

I was exhausted. I dozed off for an unknown length of time. I was awakened by the police and told the family wanted to talk. As I approached the fence, the mother asked me to come to her. She put her gloved hand on the fence and asked me to put mine to hers. She said, "We know the accident was not your fault. Reyna's sister was across the highway and yelled to her to hurry before the pickup left for the cantón. She tried to make it and lost. "God bless you and be at peace," said the mother. "We accept the $5,000 you have offered."

The negotiating had been finished and the attorney general had accepted the police report of what had happened. The only item left before they could all go home and I went to jail was for the coroner to confirm the death. The police car had been driven behind the fence with me confined in the back seat. Within a short time, another official pickup approached the hospital. A man and a woman exited and approached the two policemen who were standing in front of the garage that contained Reyna's body. But they did not go into the garage, at least not immediately. How else would they confirm her death? But the policemen talked and they listened, occasionally turning to look at me as though I was an animal in the zoo for special study. They read from the report and talked some more. After what seemed like an eternity they all went into the garage for the final confirmation of Reyna's death.

Reyna's body was loaded into the bed of the family pickup and with them surrounding her on every side as though to protect her from the cold they drove off into the dark of the night. The only piece left for the police was to take me to jail. The policeman came to the car, opened the door and said, "Go home." This time it was Daniela's turn to be surprised and for me to be grateful. Daniela asked "Why?" Of course, I did not want her to talk any more, but to be quiet, get me in the car and get me out of there. He said because I was obviously remorseful and after having talked with the attorney general's office and the coroner's office, the decision had been made I should not have to go to jail. They were certain that I would pay the $5,000 that we had negotiated as payment. There was no doubt in anyone's mind that I would show up for court to close the case, and they all were willing to defend this decision in court if need be to let me go home to sleep instead of being taken to jail. I went to Daniela's hospitality house, but I did not sleep.

Project of God

The next few days are something of a blur in my mind. The trauma of having killed Reyna, even though, logically, I felt I was not at fault, nevertheless, I carried a heavy weight of responsibility in my heart. The specifics I do recall are that Alejandro Lopez showed up at the house early the next morning and stayed with me until the entire ordeal of payment to the family, insurance report completed, the car was processed out of police custody and taken to a body shop for repair and the court order of case closed was declared. Alejandro, in that time, confirmed for me a respect and love that bound us like family. I often refer to him even today as my Salvadoran son. There was something more to be done, and he was the one to make it happen.

Alejandro

In court that took place in Cuidad Arce on a Thursday, the judge asked the family if they were satisfied with the settlement that had been made. They confirmed that they were. The judge noted that the police had expressed in their report I had been remorseful and cooperative and she was grateful that I had made the process less difficult than usual. Then she asked if I had anything else I wanted to add to the court proceedings. I said, "Yes, please."

It had been twelve days since the accident. I could not get out of my mind the wish by the family to build for the two children, now essentially orphaned, a humble home with water and electricity. In conversations with friends and Compañeros, I had suggested we should explore the possibility of making that dream come true. Everyone encouraged the exploration of the idea. And so, that day, I told the court with the family present that it was my hope to be able to put together the resources necessary to construct a three-bedroom home for the children; a room for each of them and a room for whomever would be their caregiver.

In the months that followed, I raised money from churches, family, and friends. Alejandro became the project manager and the house became a reality six months later. The grandfather of the two children donated the land and an attorney volunteered the time and talent to transfer it into Reyna's and Cristian's names so they would be owners of the home.

Don David, who lives in the Cantón Conacaste, was hired as foreman of the construction. On March 17, 2006, construction began.

I need to digress here before I describe the Project of God. If the reader has experienced tragedy then you likely know that someone will eventually tell you that the tragedy was "God's will." That is, in my opinion, a twisted sense of who God is, and it damages the spirit and sanctity of the human relationship with the Holy. If God is the author of untimely deaths, then whence comes the grace that moves the soul through it to hope and peace? God did not kill a mother in order that her two children could have a roof over their heads. Such "God's will that it happened" theology digs the pain deeper, alienates us from the belief in a loving God, and despair, even depression, take up residence in the midst of faith.

If causing Reyna's death was God's will, then that, I deduced, made me the instrument in God's hand. I did not care to accept that premise about God, or myself. Humans can do their own tragedies without God's help in making them happen. However, the journey back to a sense of wholeness for me, battling the guilt, fighting back the images of that tragic night, was not a smooth one for me. Angels did not fly in to attend to me so, for a while, it seemed the only other option was to anesthetize my mind so my soul could rest. I had lived through depression in my life. I did not care to live it again. I don't care to illuminate how I did that or with what, nor do I excuse it. But living by myself much of the time in what was to be my retirement home up the mountain in Planes de Rendero made it easy. There are, I concluded, worse things in life than addictions.

Alejandro did an excellent job of putting the pieces together for construction of the house. It evolved from building a home for the children to a Project of God when Fr. Jim Laurenzo, the priest at St. Catherine of Siena and Drake Student Center in Des Moines became involved. Jim had brought Drake University student delegations to El Salvador since 2003. He wanted them to experience the reality of poverty in developing countries and he always wanted the students to have a workday. The workday for the student delegation in 2006 was helping with constructing the home for the children in Conacaste. Even though it was nothing more than digging dirt for the footings and moving sand, he was satisfied it would be a learning experience.

Fr. Jim Laurenzo with student participants
of Drake University Delegation

The delegation arrived, and we had several days of immersion into Salvadoran life before the workdays began. I don't know how much Father Jim knew of my depression and despair, but he, having suffered his own sorts of life tragedies, I am sure suspected something was up with my emotions. Without prompting, Jim early on said to me, "Bob, God cries with you in tragedies." He debunked the "God's will" theology and suggested the only way to healing and reconciliation of my life is to let God in on the pain. On Sunday before the workday for the students, Jim celebrated Mass at the small chapel erected on the site of the senseless murder of the four American women. Considered martyrs in their community of faith, they were beaten, brutally raped, and killed by members of an El Salvadoran National Guard death squad on December 2, 1980. In that place of pain so great it likely welcomed death, pain that makes death by accident a cakewalk, Fr. Jim Laurenzo celebrated God's word of reconciliation. I believe it was where he first used the phrase "Project of God" and then applied it to the reconciliation that would occur in the building of a house the Drake students would work on the next day.

Later that day Jim asked me how we would do lunch the next day, given we would be in a cantón without restaurants. Alejandro and I had planned efficiently and we would purchase two-piece Pollo Compero chicken boxes for each of the delegation and the three workers. To which he replied, with a voice as close to anger as I have ever heard from him, "What about the community who will be there to watch? What about the children? What about the neighbors?" And so the plan for individual chicken boxes changed to the purchase of lunch meat, cheese, fruit, chips, cookies, juice, and pop--as much as $80 would buy at Super Selectos. Whoever was there would be invited to have lunch.

We arrived at the work site close to 9 a.m. Work had already begun and it consisted of moving dirt to prepare the site for footings and sand for making cement when it came time to pour them. Those who did not dig dirt began to play with the children. I noted with satisfaction that Reyna, the orphan, was enthusiastic with digging and was having a good time with the students working beside her. As the children played with students and students sweat with labor, a celebratory mood set in. When it came time to eat, some of the students set out the food and sent children to invite anyone who wanted to eat.

People came, children, women, men, young, and old. Reyna's grandfather, grandmother, aunts, and uncles came to the table. In the end more than sixty people ate and there was some food left over. Reyna's grandfather, a short, muscular man with a friendly smile, asked to speak. All who were dining on lunchmeat sandwiches turned to him as his lip began to quiver. While I cannot repeat verbatim his words, essentially this is what he said: "This morning when you all came to work, I was embarrassed. For we are so poor and I did not think there was anything you could do that would be of help. But I watched you, the young people, sweating as you moved dirt and heavy sand. You never complained. And those who did not have a shovel played with our children. They had a good time and you showed them love." Then he looked at Jim and said, "You brought everyone food. Everyone had something to eat and there is even some food left over. Today Jesus came to our house." That day something renewed in my soul. The dark night turned to dawn and spring set in where winter had brought death. "Project of God." It took nearly five months to finish building the house. Their father came home from Mexico sometime during the construction and now is living with his children. The house is bigger than it needed to be. The children were so used to sleeping in the same room that they put their beds together in one bedroom. I bought them bunk beds so Beatris, their cousin of the same age, also sleeps in the house. But it is a good house and well used by several of the family and that is the way of Salvadoran families. They share when they have more than they need and others have less than they need.

The Project of God House built for
Reyna and Cristian, children of Reyna Marisol

The Multiplication Beyond the Sharing of Food

At this point of the experience of life out of death, one could say that is a good story. Yes, you could say that, and it is. Children have a home they never dreamed of having. Their father is living with them again. They have education promised for as long as they want to go to school, initiated by a $2,000 fund given by Lois Crilly, and to which I am committed to continuing for as long as they want to go to school, including the university, if that is their choice. But there was still more. A church was built and finished in November, 2009, replacing the one that was destroyed in the earthquake of 2001. Each year as the Drake students continued their annual trip to El Salvador to learn about Third World poverty, they also made a project in Conacaste a part of their work day. In 2007, they painted the school, and in 2008, they built latrines for the poor. By 2009 the church was the focus of their daily work. The parish of St. Catherine of Siena, led by Fr. Jim Laurenzo, who also led the student delegations, felt the spirit of relationship and began to ask what it could mean for their parish beyond student delegations from Drake. Why should the students have all the fun? parish delegations began to visit Conacaste. They met with the education directiva, the community directiva, and the church directiva and discussed with them their hopes and needs for the community. Jim celebrated Mass in their makeshift dirt-floor, tin-roof church with no sides and few pews for worship. As questions of need were raised, there was a universal expression by all the community leadership that a church would renew their sense of community and provide a place not only for worship, but also for health care promotion and social events. At this writing, and before I ever finish these memoirs, the Cantón Conacaste has a new brick, tile-floor majestic church built with financial and moral support from the St. Catherine of Siena parish in Des Moines, Iowa. It is not my story, and even if I wrote it, an entire chapter would have to be devoted to the many decision-making moments and fundraising events and delegation visits that brought it to reality. Fr. Jim and Margaret and Jack Cavanagh are saints that set that Project of God into motion.

It is their story and I am grateful that the parish allowed me to travel with them as their guide each time they made the trip to El Salvador. Thank you. It has been a wonderful ride.

A Postscript on Death in El Salvador

I saw a group of women running from the market area toward the clinic. As they got closer, I could see the older of them carrying a bundle. She held it close to her breast as though to protect it from harm, and her eyes darted from the bundle to people in the street as though she was looking for someone or something. I stood on the sidewalk and tried to make sense of the scene that was unfolding before me. As the group got closer, I recognized the older woman and the younger ones with her as her sisters and daughters. I could see their tear-filled eyes. They saw me and suddenly, with grief that rose to wailing, they paused before me.

The woman holding the bundle offered it to me and, in that moment, I became aware that their grief was for a baby wrapped in a tattered blanket. I could see the baby and that, if he or she was not dead, the infant was very near death. I felt a sense of deep sadness that I cannot adequately describe. It was as though the mother hoped that I, a gringo, with the power of the first world, who had come to their pueblo to live among them, could do something miraculous just because I was who I am. Maybe I had resources that were unavailable to poor people like her. Quickly she understood that I, too, was helpless. She pulled the baby to her breast and continued running to the clinic a block away. She wanted a miracle. All I could do was hope that the doctors would be able to perform the miracle she sought from me. An hour later the slow toll of the church bell announced to the community that there had been a death. I knew it was the baby in the tattered blanket that she had offered up to me in desperate hope of mercy.

In a short time after moving to Berlin in 2001, it became obvious that death was a common occurrence in the pueblo. It happened so often that I quickly became aware of a defining culture of death. All societies have such an ethos. But this culture was different from the one I had grown up with and lived in the rural Midwest of the United States. In all that time the only dead people I ever saw were in a casket, dressed as if ready for church. The only exception to this rule that I can recall is my own father. You see, my father always wore overalls, as though dressed for work. I never recall seeing him in anything remotely resembling a Sunday-go-to-meeting suit. Thus, it just made sense for him to be dressed in what he always wore every day for his funeral.

So death became something of a culture shock for me when I moved from the U.S. to El Salvador. Death was ever-present, just like the poverty. One can touch it, smell it, and get close to it. I remember the first person I saw lying on the highway, someone struck by a car that continued on its way without stopping to consider administering aid. They probably thought they were doing the corpse a favor, and certainly avoiding legal complications in a county in which everything is legally complicated. I also remember the first murdered person I saw, surrounded by police tape while the investigation was proceeding. And there were the several friends of the pastoral team, with whom I worked, and whose wakes I attended. Over time I came to attend the wakes of babies, of young adults, and older people. These people are closer to death than are the people in the First World. They know death as personal, and they live in its constant presence and likelihood, daily. Imagine laying out Grandpa Ed on your dining room table and having family and close friends come for an evening of condolences, coffee, and sweet bread. We clean death up to make is proper and sanitary. In El Salvador, prayers and rosaries are recited, and the support of friends and family lasts long into the night and the days to come. The death is everybody's in a unique way. The next day the body is placed in a simple casket and hoisted on the shoulders of loved ones, or put into a pickup truck, for the trip to the cemetery, mourners following on foot. The family and friends fill the grave and stay until the task is completed. From wake to internment, it is a 24-hour celebration of life.

Every November 1, the Day of the Dead, families gather in the cemetery to cut grass on the graves of their loved ones. Many plant flowers and paint the tomb stone while socializing with others around them. In the Latino culture the dead are given special attention and are not forgotten.

Chapter 9

Woman in the Blue Dress

"Let your love be continuous. Never forget to show kindness to strangers, for by such kindness, some have actually entertained angels unaware."
Book of Hebrews 13.2

Traveling in El Salvador can be an adventure. From the beaches to the mountains there are unknown roads to travel. The time of civil war from 1980 to 1992 brought political and social isolation to some parts of the country, especially in the northern and eastern parts. The isolation and division caused by war brought suspicion of strangers who arrived unannounced. So I usually traveled with other Salvadorans to feel safe and beyond the reach of the unknown lurking in the roads being traveled. On occasion, circumstances brought travel alone. There was one such occasion in 1992 I remember well. It was the month just after signing the peace accords that ended the long civil war. It truly was a trek into the unknown, and it embraced an adventure some would say was guided by a guardian angel. Others would chalk it up to coincidence. I know what I think, and I will leave to the reader his or her own conclusion.

The old thirty-passenger Bluebird school bus lumbered along with its overload of at least fifty passengers. I was traveling with Judy Anderson, a friend from Des Moines, and a Drake University student who had just graduated. They both had heard me speak about El Salvador and decided they wanted in on the experience. We planned a month-long foray into various parts of El Salvador, including an extended stay in El Tablón, the cantón that brought me to El Salvador in the first place. A woman from California who had taken a delegation to San Jose de Las Flores was staying at the Lutheran Guest House in San Salvador where we were, and she told us a trip there was a must. So we packed an overnight bag and boarded a bus to find the place she talked about.

San Jose de Las Flores is in the northern part of El Salvador in the state of Chalatenango. It was the first repopulation community during the war. Its citizens had been massacred in the early 1980s, and survivors had fled to a refugee camp in nearby Honduras. In the mid-1980s they decided to return to their homes even though they were always under threat of attack by the U.S. supported Salvadoran military. The woman from California had talked about a well-organized community, and that a trip there would help us understand the reality that the people had lived with during the war. I already had a sense of that reality from my first trip when I stayed sixteen days and nights in El Tablón. But Judy was quite interested, and I yearned to know other parts of the country. So we boarded the bus that would take us to the city of Chalatenango. From there we would find our way to San Jose de Las Flores.

Lesson number #1: It is never wise to assume anything about traveling in a Third World nation, especially that all buses travel to all cantóns and pueblos.

Here ends the lesson.

There is a man on each bus called a "cobra," and he is responsible for collecting the fare from each person who boards the bus. The number of people on the bus was such that three people were put on seats intended for two and the aisle was filled with people standing. I was seated between two women, one in a blue dress. I had wiggled to pull the colones from my front pants pocket to pay for the fare, and instead of trying to put the change I received from the cobra in my pocket, I dropped it in a basket that the woman with the blue dress was holding on her lap. It was only centavos de Colon (cents of a colon, which was the currency of that time in El Salvador); still she smiled and nodded in her gratitude.

The bus traveled through the sugar cane area of Colima with mountains of Chalatenango rising in the distance. Soon after we crossed over the mouth of the Embalse Cerrón Grande, an engineered reservoir, the bus made a sharp right turn into the mountains of Chalatenango. The bus made frequent stops to take on new passengers and to allow others to disembark. Passengers pushed through the narrow aisle filled with people, crates of chickens, baskets of vegetables, and cartons tied with red, yellow, and green rope that made travel even slower than normal. So by the time we reached the city Chalatenango, it was late in the afternoon.

Being the only gringos on the bus made us feel rather conspicuous. If the color of our skin was not enough of a dead giveaway, the overnight bags over the shoulder and bottles of water clutched in our hands were certainly the *pièce de résistance*. The bus parked on a narrow street, and the cobra announced we had arrived in Chalatenango, and that we should disembark. I felt certain the information was given specifically for the gringos.

The woman in the blue dress disembarked ahead of us. She moved through the crowd to a place on the sidewalk and motioned for us to come. She was a short woman, not much more than four feet tall. The dress was a brilliant blue that had been faded by numerous washings and drying in the sun. The woman's sun-wrinkled face wore a kind smile, and she asked us where we were headed. We told her San José de Las Flores, and inquired which bus and when it departed. That is when we learned there was no bus from Cuidad Chalatenango to San José de Las Flores. Even though San José de Las Flores had become a well-known community and visited by delegations on a regular basis, the government of El Salvador was not about to provide decent transportation for its citizens, let alone a well constructed road. She explained the only vehicle transportation available was by pickups that are for hire to haul passengers. She led us to the point on the northern edge of the city where pickups stopped for fare-paying people. She looked to the sun that was low in the sky and suggested to us that it was too late to make the trip. So she took us to a local hotel that cost three dollars per night and suggested it would not be wise for us to venture outside the hotel after dark. We shook bugs from the single sheet that covered the well-used mattresses and gave thanks that we had packed fruit and bread in the overnight bag that now was going to become a two-night bag. It all began to feel surreal, and the wisdom of even having embarked on the trip began to be in question. An exclamation point to the ridiculousness of our situation was made when the young Drake graduate was shocked to the floor when she reached to turn on the single bulb light. We opted for candlelight to illuminate our way for the rest of the evening.

The rooster crows of the early morning woke us to the rising sun and cold-water baths. We found a restaurant close by for beans and eggs, and we soon were on our way to the location to wait for a pickup to carry us to San José de Las Flores. It was a truck instead of a pickup that slowed to a stop, but transportation is transportation, so we climbed into the back and settled in for the ride ahead. The woman in the blue dress had told us it was about an hour ride from Chalatenango to San José de Las Flores, so when the truck slowed to a stop within half an hour, we were surprised. The driver said he was taking the fork to the right and that the road we were to take went to the left. He told us we should be careful whom we take rides from and, with those words of caution echoing in our minds, we watched the truck roar away with its huge tires making a cloud of dust that soon hid the vehicle from sight.

The road to the left was the less traveled, with grass growing between two worn tire tracks. Dust was thick, and each step made a foot impression like snow does in winter in Iowa. We walked single-file without much conversation except an occasional retort of how long we would have to walk before a ride was offered. The sun was strong on our heads, and I wished silently I had brought a larger bottle of water and a smaller overnight bag. No need to panic, I thought. Not yet anyway. And so we walked, each to our own thoughts about the reality we had encountered.

Then from the side of the road, through the thicket that lined the ditches, came the same woman in the blue dress that we had encountered the day before, appearing as if from nowhere. She had directed us to a hotel for the night. She had shown us where to catch pickup transportation to San José de Las Flores. Now here she was again, a half hour from Chalatenango to give us directions once again. She smiled at us, but it was not enough to cover the chastising she gave us for our poor planning. Her scolding was easily borne, because we were so happy to see her, and her blue dress was a welcome sight. My spirits were buoyed when she took the lead and began to walk with us. I was confident this woman of short stature was our salvation from any threat of danger. The road to San José de Las Flores just became much more friendly and welcoming.

I learned early on, and it was in my mind at that moment, that El Salvador can be a fearsome place. Violence had ruled since the Spanish Inquisition, and the poor had always the violence of hunger, with just enough to manage to live through one more day, and hope the next one would be better. Since my first visit to El Salvador in 1990, my consciousness about a long history of violence in all Latin America had surfaced so that I was constantly aware of impending doom around the next curve or outside the bolted door, where I went to sleep at sundown, because there was no light to read by. And it was not safe to venture beyond the bolted door in the dark. The civil war had just ended and there were constant reminders of the history of doom that the country lived with its entire existence that continued just under the surface of hope in what they were calling the peace accords when the war ended.

I focused my attention on the woman in the blue dress. This pixie of a person was my source of comfort out in the middle of a Salvadoran tree-lined and little traveled road. She held her head high, like an ear to the ground, to listen for noise that may alert her to oncoming traffic, traffic that might possibly represent a friend or, perhaps because of the historic poverty that ravages the human spirit, a vehicle might well spell our doom incarnated in a pickup load of angry young men whom poverty had ravaged just one day too long. She was alert as to what lie ahead. She frequently turned around to survey her gringo "army" who somehow misplaced their rational thinking and had wound up on the edge of an unknown and hostile territory that could turn on them at any moment.

But it didn't. She heard it first and moved us to the side of the road, watching behind for the vehicle that was approaching. Hopeful eyes with cautious expression on her face kept watch on the curve until what appeared to be an official car, of what or whom I am not sure, that came into view. Her face relaxed and she put out her hand as she moved to the middle of the road to flag the vehicle down. After a short conversation, she gained permission for us to enter, along with her, and thus we received a ride to our destination. When we arrived in the community, she sought out someone she knew so we would

The Woman/Angel in the Blue Dress

receive hospitality for the night we were there. Then she walked away down the road from which we had come. She turned back toward us and with a stern look betrayed by the twinkle of her eye that told us to behave and stay inside at night. Then she disappeared, like an angel of unknown origin, into the mysterious unknown of the thicket-lined dusty road.

It was lunchtime so we searched out the local restaurant. There we encountered our second Waterloo, the first being the transportation fiasco just getting there. It is so much the way we think as Americans, that naturally people would welcome gringo strangers into their community, lacking any invitation and expecting warm and open arms. I am embarrassed when I think about it now. They had lived through a massacre in the early 1980s, and then day after day of war after repopulating the community they had been driven from. The ink on the signed peace accords ending the civil war was not even dry yet and there we were waltzing into their community life without invitation or even announcement that we were coming. How very gringo and rude and, might I add, dangerous. So there we were, munching on pupusas and sipping beer when a tall, ruddy complexioned man entered and without pause, said in a heavy European accent, "Vat dar chew doin hair?" And he did not smile when he said it. My diplomatic skills ultimately won out and when he understood we were just tourists trying to learn the reality of the poor and those who had suffered through the war he smiled and said we were welcome. And that, in fact, he would be honored to show us around.

"My name is Rafael," he said, "and I was a sniper for the FMLN during the war." He had come from Switzerland early in the war and joined the revolutionary army for the duration. He proudly showed us the rehabilitation project for disabled revolutionaries who had lost limbs in the war. Then he said, "Let's go for a walk." It turned out to be about a four-mile walk into the fields and forests surrounding the pueblo to the FMLN encampment. It was so well hidden that we did not know it was there until we were almost upon it. It was a large area that included a kitchen, bunkhouse, and hospital. Here was proof that the revolutionary army that had been described by the Salvadoran and U.S. governments as drug-running delinquents was actually a very organized and trained army that fought its way to victory. That revolutionary army today is one of the two major political parties in El Salvador, the FMLN Party. We found ourselves in the midst of the El Salvadoran George Washingtons or Thomas Jeffersons of their time and community.

The next morning Rafael was at the pickup that would take us back to Chalatenango, where we would catch the bus to San Salvador. He said thanks for coming, and call first next time. I reminded him there were no telephones in the community. He looked at me and said, "You figure it out." That was another example in my Salvadoran experience that reminded me I am not an island, and there are organizations that are in solidarity through which I could plan and work.

The overloaded pickup truck ride from San José de Las Flores cost us each five colones, about sixty cents. We got out at the same place we had caught the truck the day before on our way to the community. The way to the bus that would take us to San Salvador was about a five-block walk, and as we made our way through the crowded streets of the city, I felt a hand on my arm. There next to me was, unbelievably, the woman in the blue dress. She walked with us without saying a word to make sure we found the correct bus. We boarded and found a seat. I watched out the window as she disappeared into the crowd. Up to that time, I never gave much credence to the existence of angels, and since I have never ceased believing.

Chapter 10

Get Out of Jail Free Card

The night before Herod was to bring him to trial, Peter was asleep, in prison, bound with chains, and sentries stood guard at the entrance. Suddenly an angel of the Lord appeared and a light shone in the cell. The angel woke Peter, saying, "Quick, get up!" and the chains fell off Peter's wrists. The angel said to him, "Gather your clothing and sandals and follow me." Peter followed the angel out of the prison, still having no idea that what the angel was doing was really happening; believing it may be a dream or vision. They passed all the security, walked out through the guarded gate and he was free.
Book of Acts. 12.6ff

I sat on a hard bench in an immigration office somewhere in Mexico on the road to Chiapas. The immigration officer had my passport and keys to the pickup, and I was being detained for transporting an illegal from El Salvador. It was true that Erica was in my pickup when we were stopped at the immigration check-point on the Pan American Highway two hours north of the Mexico-Guatemalan border. That I was intentionally transporting someone from El Salvador without papers was far from the truth. My language skills failed to communicate to the immigration officer how this had happened and slowly my fears set in that maybe I would face prison for this or worse, be deported to the U.S. with denial of traveling back to my missionary home in Berlin, El Salvador. I could not recall a time in my life when I felt as angry as I did at that moment toward Erica for putting me in the situation I was in.

It had begun two months before when she came to the parish team house in Berlin, looking for me. She had a note from her brother, who lived in Des Moines and whose children I had baptized several years before. The note read: "Brother Robert, help my sister if you can, please. She would like to come to the United States." As Erica explained the note, she claimed she had been denied a visa from the U.S. Embassy in San Salvador and she wanted to find a way to get there without a visa. I told her as gently as I could that I did not, could not, and most emphatically would not help her organize her trip to illegally travel to the U.S. I went on to say that if she would get papers to travel in Mexico, I would be visiting friends in Chiapas, Mexico, in the next couple months and she could ride with me that far. The rest of the trip would be up to her. A few weeks later she called and said she was ready to go and to let her know when I was leaving. We left together two weeks later for the trip to Chiapas.

We left Berlin in the parish team's 1989 Toyota four-wheel drive pickup on a Sunday. I listened to her tell the story why she had to get to the U.S. She and her two children lived with her elderly parents. Her resources were limited, and while they had food and a roof over their heads, she was unable to pay the cost of education, let alone decent clothing for her children. As we traveled, our conversation that reflected her hopes for a better life with money earned in the U.S. made me feel deeply that the part I was playing in getting her there was correct, and just as important, legal.

We entered Guatemala from El Salvador and new rules of traveling from one country to another in Central America made it unnecessary for Erica to process through. But she was told and she acknowledged she needed a visa at the Mexican border. I had my passport stamped to enter Guatemala and we drove on, through Guatemala City, past Antigua, and Panajachel to Xela, where we were able to finally find a motel for the night. I figured that was about half way to Chiapas and with an early start on Monday morning, we could be there by mid-afternoon. Over a dinner of pupusas, rice, and beans I listened to Erica muse about how finally she would be able to provide a better life for her children and her only concern was how she would get across at the U.S. border.

We were up early to continue the trip to Chiapas and found ourselves at the Mexican border by mid-morning. It was a lengthy process for me at immigration, as I not only had to get a visa for Mexico but I also had to register the pickup and pay a tax for driving on Mexican roads. It took at least an hour and a half and when I exited the building, I found Erica sitting on the pickup running board reading a pamphlet she had been given by an evangelical who was nearby shouting salvation to all who would give their heart to Jesus. I asked her if she was finished with immigration and she said she was, and we were ready to enter Mexico. As I eased the pickup onto the highway and settled in for the rest of the drive, Erica told me, "I have something I must tell you." I thought maybe she was going to launch into another conversation about how happy she was to be making the trip. Or maybe she had to go to the bathroom. But what I heard caused my heart to leap to my throat. She said, and I will never forget her exact words, *"No tengo yo una visa y más no tengo un pasaporte."* (I don't have a visa, and I don't have a passport). That made her illegal in Mexico and there she was in my pickup. So the truth was she never did try to get a visa to the U.S., which was her story when I first met her, and the reason she had decided to go without one. But she didn't because you cannot apply for one without a passport. I had been duped by her lie and her damsel in distress act. I slowed the pickup and began to think about the possible consequences and what I should do. Maybe I should turn around and take her back to the border for her to find her own way. My mind raced with considerations, but before I could make a decision we came upon five Mexican soldiers who waved us to the shoulder of the highway. I was relieved when they asked where we were headed and then said they had to search the vehicle for guns but did not ask for passports from us. They searched thoroughly the entire pickup, under the hood and our luggage and then told us to go on with a wish that we have a good trip. That experience encouraged me that maybe we would have no problem with the visa requirement. So I decided to drive on toward Chiapas.

We passed police checkpoints without being stopped. Each pueblo we passed through put us closer to our destination and I began to relax and anticipate our arrival in Chiapas. Then as suddenly as a rattle snake striking its victim, there out in the middle of nowhere a detour in the road appeared. Next to it was a sign that said, "Immigration checkpoint." An officer in a blue uniform approached my window and asked for passports. I produced mine. After asking Erica three times for hers she looked at me and said to him, "I don't have one." The officer said to me, "Park the pickup over there," pointing a finger to a parking space near a small cement block building. "Then give me your keys and passport and come inside. You are a coyote running an illegal. We know how you work, thinking we will let a single person through with a gringo at the wheel." I knew what I heard but did not want to believe it. Everything seemed to move in slow motion and my mind raced with what the consequences of Erica's lie would be. My life as I knew it seemed to be going down the tube and I felt lost and without hope.

The look of the immigration officer was stern as he recorded my passport number in a ledger he had on a small wooden desk. He made a telephone call from a phone that was sitting on the same desk and had a lengthy conversation without looking at me. His speech was rapid and I could not follow the theme of his conversation. When he hung up, I asked what would happen to us. He said Erica would be deported back to the Salvadoran border. As for me, he was not sure.

In the next half hour as I waited for the decision of what would happen to me, the immigration officer received two phone calls. Each time I thought he would have information about my destiny. Each time he put the phone down and went back to writing in the ledger where he had recorded my passport number. "I have to go to the bathroom," Erica announced and he directed her to a door in the corner of the room. She was gone for five minutes, then ten. I wondered if there was a window in the bathroom though which she had escaped. I was relieved when she finally exited and sat down next to me on the hard wooden bench. What happened next put me into another "slow motion" moment.

I heard the immigration officer's voice, but what I heard couldn't be true. I must have misunderstood. He called me over to his desk and began to draw a map that would bypass other immigration checkpoints on the way to Chiapas. He said we should take the road that intersected with the Pan American Highway that would take us through four cantóns. He drew them on a map, putting the name next to each one. We would come out on the Pan American Highway and we could continue on to Chiapas. Then he said, and it rings in my ears to this day, "*Se van ahorita y te manejas la via dije yo.*" ("Leave now and drive the route I told you.") I couldn't believe it. I offered him a hundred pesos, and he said he wanted no payment. Then he became rather urgent that we should leave immediately.

He gave me the keys and my passport and watched us go. As we departed he said, "*Que le vaya bien.*" ("Go the way of good"). With the same urgency with which he announced we should leave, I sped off in the direction he had instructed us to go. When we were well out of sight of the immigration stop, I pulled to the side of the highway and tried to calm my nerves that were raw and on edge. I felt I had just missed a bad accident or bad news had really been nothing but a dream. Then Erica said with a smirk on her face, "I didn't need to go to the bathroom back there. I just wanted a private space where I could get down on my knees and pray to God to soften that man's heart." I have thought often about that experience and, try as I might, I cannot think of any reason that man would have changed his mind, except for God's intervention that softened his heart. I thank God for what I think of as "my get out of jail free" card.

There is one more experience of the trip to Chiapas that gives me pause to consider God's presence with us on that trip. We drove through the four cantónes and came to the Pan American highway as he suggested we would. I turned left onto to the highway and there, no more than fifty yards ahead was a road block with more soldiers than I could count waiting to check vehicles. My heart raced as I approached the stop. The soldier at the gate looked at the Salvadoran license plate, and then he read the sign on the door of the pickup that said, "Equipo Pastoral, Berlin." (Pastoral Team, Berlin) With that he lifted the arm and said to us, "Welcome to Mexico, El Salvador. Have a good trip, Father." He assumed I was a priest, and I told him no different as I increased our speed to put distance between the contingency of soldiers checking vehicles, and our vehicle.

We made it to Chiapas without further incident. I vowed then I would never drive anyone without first seeing their papers and knowing they are legal to be in that country. God has better things to do, I believe, than to watch out for fools who don't.

Chapter 11

Claudia Nadina's Miracle

"My Lord God, I have no idea where I am going. I do not see the road ahead of me. I cannot know for certain where it will end... but I believe that the desire to please you does in fact please you. And I hope that I have that desire in all that I am doing... Therefore will I trust you always though I may seem to be lost and in the shadow of death... You will never leave me to face my perils alone."
Thomas Merton

By 2001, when I moved to Berlin to live, people in the pueblo had been exposed to a number of visits by delegations from Iowa. The first medical delegation that arrived in 1997 and every year since from First Presbyterian church in Newton had provided a considerable number of health exams as well as donations of medicine.

Perhaps the most celebrated was the Presbytery of Des Moines' dedication to bringing Milagro Granados, a young woman with foot problems, to Des Moines for surgery. Dr. Jeffrey Farber, an Orthopedic Surgeon in Des Moines, had donated the surgical skill and Blank Hospital provided the post-surgical care. Joyce and Jim Hoffman from Heartland Presbyterian Church in Clive opened their home for three months of hospitality for Miligro and her mother Haydee during the healing time. And though the surgery had not totally corrected Milagro's problem with walking pigeon-toed, at least she could walk long distances that she could not do before. So requests for medical care were quite common and when Angela, who runs a vegetable and fruit stand in the market with her husband Salvador, asked if I would assist a friend's daughter find a transplanta de medula I was quick to say "yes." With my limited Spanish capability I had interpreted her request to help with finding a blood transfusion. What she was really asking for was help finding a bone marrow transplant as a cure for the young woman's leukemia. So began my journey of faith with Claudia Nadina Hernandez to find a cure for her leukemia. She calls me "papa." She was 20 years old. This is the story.

Claudia's doctor is director of the cancer hospital in San Salvador. His name is Dr. Valencia. I sometimes accompanied Claudia on her journey for weekly medical appointments, leaving Berlin by bus at 4:30 a.m. and, when Casa Pastoral later acquired a pick up, at 5:30 a.m., to be in San Salvador at the lab in time for an early morning blood exam. Then we waited for a few hours until her appointment time, which was anytime Dr. Valencia could see her between 9 a.m. and noon. He is a compassionate man and speaks some English, so I was able to understand more or less the process (or lack of it) Claudia was making. He lamented the lack of resources the hospital had to work with, and the desire to find a source for obtaining Gleevec, the newest medicine that was marketed by a U.S. pharmaceutical company. He lamented even more the denial for free Gleevec he had received from the Max Foundation, which is set up to provide free medicine to patients in need in Latin America. The foundation was the only known source at the time for hope of providing the medicine that cost $2,650 per month per patient.

I concentrated on finding a bone marrow transplant for Claudia. The old adage "ignorance is bliss" was applicable. And any hope I had as I began the journey into the unknown of medicine to find a bone marrow transplant was smashed when I learned the cost of one would be between $150,000 and $300,000.00 when done in the United States. Strike one.

It immediately became clear that I was out of my league, in both knowledge of medicine and finding necessary financial resources to pay such a large amount. Faith was my only resource and prayer was the expression of hope in faith. I prayed for a resource, a place to begin, and a reason to maintain the promise I had made to the request to help find a bone marrow transplant. I had spent enough time with Claudia that I knew she did not hold me responsible to be the answer to her medical needs, but still my persistence held out hope for her. She began in that time to call me papa, which expressed a love and appreciation that drove me to explore all options, no matter how remote the possibility to succeed in the quest.

Tom Carney is a friend and supporter of Latin America causes. He also at the time was Assistant to the Director of the Iowa Department of Health. It was a presumptuous thing to request from Tom, yet I knew he would understand. And, besides, God guides the process so I sent an email to him, asking if he knew of any resources I could explore for a bone marrow transplant for Claudia. Within hours of the sending of my message to Tom, I received a response. He knew of no resources but would send a mass email to people in the medical field to see what might surface. From that mass email I received one response. It was from Dr. Richard Boxer, a physician from Milwaukee. In a very brief message he said Claudia needed Gleevec. It was her best chance for a cure. It was what we already knew. It was what Dr. Valencia had tried to get from Max Foundation and the request was denied.

Reality has a way of making a situation desperate. It had been a year since the request for help had come from Angela to help Claudia. In that year we had learned that Gleevec was an option for a cure, but it was out of reach at $2,650 per month as was the $300,000 for a bone marrow transplant. Prayer was the single solitary source of hope, and even that was beginning to feel dead-end. Then in on March 4, 2003, the walk of faith took an unexpected turn. I found myself on a plane on the way to Havana, Cuba, by way of Panama to seek a bone marrow transplant there.

I had been with Claudia's family as they talked with a young man in San Salvador about Cuba. He had been there and knew the hospital, where to stay, and what the cost would be for expenses. He believed it was possible for Claudia to receive a bone marrow transplant at a cost far-reduced from the quoted $300,000. It was not until the day Claudia was to leave that I learned that the family wanted me, not Claudia's

Aunt Stella, to go with her. It would be my task to negotiate for Claudia with doctors in Cuba for a bone marrow transplant. It was the gringo image. They felt it gave me more negotiating power than they had. I felt honored, but also filled with apprehension and fear. For one thing, my Spanish language skills were far from fluent. In addition, no one knew we were coming. So began an adventure to Cuba, where it is against the law for U.S. citizens to travel because of the U.S. embargo against Cuba that has been in place since the Castro led revolution in 1948. For reading material I took with me "Farewell to Arms" by Ernest Hemingway. It seemed a fitting book to read while I was in Cuba, as he lived some of his life there and that is also where he ended his life. The stark reality of his writings along with his own journey of life spoke volumes to me as I embarked on an unlawful journey that could result in a $25,000 fine by the U.S. State Department for violating the long-standing embargo.

We arrived in Cuba on March 6, 2003, at 11:15 p.m. The process through immigration was full of security measures. My carry-on bag was opened after going through X-ray. I was searched bodily after going through a metal detector. The process was efficient and the workers friendly. I was interrogated for several minutes about the purpose for my trip to Cuba. Finally we were allowed to enter the country with a visa stamped on paper that would be returned to Cuban Immigration upon my departure.

We took a taxi to the Hotel William Solen that had been recommended by the young man in San Salvador who was our source of information for this trip. There were no rooms available. The taxi driver knew of some private rooms that were not legal but that Cuban citizens used as extra income source, but there also were no vacancies. The only option was for us to go to the city about ten miles away for a hotel room. We found a room at a hotel that was badly in need of repair as were buildings around it. But the room itself was quite well kept and comfortable. The cost for a night was $50 per person. The taxi cost us $40. We were already $100 over our budgeted expenses and it was only the first day of our trip. The worst was yet to come.

The next morning we rose early from a fitful sleep to a delicious breakfast that was included in the cost of the room. Then we found a taxi to take us to the hospital where Claudia would seek medical treatment for her leukemia. We pulled up in front of a large multi-floor building that could have been a warehouse for all we knew. It was badly in need of paint and some windows broken and boarded up in need of replacement. We entered what appeared to be the main door and found a large high-ceiling hallway with no one present to direct us. We walked in the direction where we heard conversation. Around a corner and down some well-worn stairs. we found a friendly janitor who guided us in person to the Office of International Medicine. We were received by a receptionist who listened to Claudia tell her story, about the man who had informed us of the hospital and possibility of services and our hope to find a bone marrow transplant while here. She listened intently, took notes, and then after hearing the story. made a couple phone calls and searched a file, looking for information about the young man from San Salvador who had recommended we come there. About an hour later. the receptionist suggested we return later in the day. The medical personnel would be ready then to begin Claudia's exam.

That was it? Claudia had provided proof of identification and records of her treatment by Dr. Valencia, and mentioned our referral to come here by a young man whose name I don't know. But there had been no questions about insurance or finances or who would be responsible for payment of the bill when we were finished. They knew Claudia was from El Salvador and she still was received with the same interest and kindness as a Cuban citizen. As we were leaving the Office of International Medicine, someone asked where we were staying. After learning of our plight the night before and the cost of the hotel where we wound up she called the Hotel William Solen and made arrangements for a double room at a $35 cost, which included breakfast. It was the same hotel where we were told the night before there were no vacancies and would not be for a few days. What we did not know is that the hotel is for patients receiving medical treatment at the Havana hospitals, and had we told them that the night before it would have saved us a bundle of money. We returned to that same office at 2 p.m. and after a brief exam of Claudia, we were told to return at 9:30 a.m. the next day to begin major tests.

Friday, March 7

When we arrived at the hospital, the nurse took Claudia to continue her exam and I was directed to another office to talk with an administrator about the cost of Claudia's exam and treatment. So there would be a cost after all. The woman behind the desk apologized profusely for the cost but all international patients were asked to pay. The fee was $80.00! I returned to the hotel for the money and waited until mid-afternoon to return to the hospital, for it was when I had been told I should be available to talk with doctors about Claudia's examinations.

When I arrived, an office assistant was waiting to take me to the area where Claudia was receiving her medical exams. We went down a long, dingy hallway badly in need of painting, through large, heavy wooden doors that opened into a bright, clean, bustling medical clinic. It was obvious the budget did not allow for maintenance, but nothing was spared for the actual medical treatment and exam areas. I was ushered into a small exam room where two doctors, a man and a woman, were waiting. In broken English, the female doctor explained that there were no matches available for Claudia to receive a bone marrow transplant, neither among Claudia's family nor within the bone marrow transplant pool of Cuba. She proposed we begin a regime of Gleevec immediately. After six months of treatment, they would examine the possibility of an auto-transplant, using Claudia's own bone marrow for the procedure. No, Gleevec was not available in Cuba for Claudia's treatment. And so we were back where we were to begin with before we made the trip to Cuba. But it had confirmed the need for Gleevec in Claudia's quest for treatment and a cure.

We had two days before our reservations to return to El Salvador. We had spent quite a lot more money than had been planned, so I kept an eye out of an ATM machine as we walked to the market to purchase some fruit and bread. There was a limited selection of all food in the market, and we learned food was always limited because of the embargo that had been placed on their country since Castro won the revolution in 1948 and the land had been declared Communist by the United States. And, of course, many U.S. allies followed suit and established an embargo on all goods to Cuba.

Given the scarcity of food, we felt it would be wrong for us to buy much, so Claudia and I each purchased an orange and a mango. I counted our money and figured with the hotel costs, taxi and exit tax at the airport we were short about $150. On the way to the hotel, we stopped at an open-air market where there was an ATM next to an ice cream stand. The ATM machine spit out a receipt that read, "transaction not permitted." I was a bit chagrined, as I knew I had several hundred dollars in the bank but a repeat try resulted with the same response. So we bought ice cream and inquired where there would be another ATM that was in working order. The woman dishing up mounds of delicious looking chocolate and coconut ice cream commented the machine worked just a few minutes ago and asked, "What bank is your credit card with?" First American Bank, I responded. She looked puzzled that was replaced with a grin, and she said, "That's a gringo card, isn't it? That is what the embargo does to us in every way every day." I would not be able to get money on my credit card because the embargo did not permit it. No American resources allowed on the island by edict of the U.S. government!

In my journal from that trip, I found written this entry in the late morning of March 7:

"I feel like an ugly American in this country, because of what my government does to the people here. Their comforts are few because of the embargo. Not much food in the market. They share jobs and make from $6 to $1,700 per month!!!!! We are running out of money and when I went to the machine to use my credit card, I was denied money because it was issued in the U.S. and the embargo does not allow its use. Claudia will call her Aunt Stella in San Salvador and ask her to send the money overnight by DHL. In the meantime, we are 'strangers in a strange land' with no resources to get home. So it goes."

One does not consider what effect an embargo has on the people of a targeted country. It has no direct effect on us and so the difficulties of its application are not understood by most. Well, by the following day of the above entry, I was in major panic from affects of the embargo the U.S. has on Cuba. Not only could I not get money from an ATM machine with my American-issued credit card, neither could we receive money overnight by DHL from El Salvador which participates in the

When The Sun Comes Up in the West

embargo. Nor could money be sent by Western Union from El Salvador, and, of course, it is impossible to send money to Cuba by any means from the United States.

Without resources to get out of Cuba, Pilar, a friend of Claudia's Aunt Stella who lives in Cuba, saved us from destitution. She put together a loan of $150 pooled by several friends of hers. It was what made it possible for us to pay the exit tax and leave the country.

Pilar also took us on a tour of the Old City of Havana. It is a beautiful, historic, and romantic place. What I saw dispelled the myth that Cuba is a "godless country." The churches and numerous restored buildings are beautiful. The statue of Christ overlooking the harbor is magnificent, the lighthouse that beacons ocean travelers, the haunts of Hemingway, and much more beckon me to return. And I will. The most touching gesture of friendship came from Letie and Sahlie, two waitresses at the hotel where we stayed. They gave me a handkerchief and Claudia lipstick and shampoo. They make $6 per month. Need I say more about the kindness of Cuban citizens?

Exiting Cuba was as much an interrogation as when entering the country. The person in immigration was friendly but firm, and asked the reason for my trip, where I live, why I live in El Salvador rather than my native country. Then she took the paper on which my visa had been stamped when I entered the country and gave me a parting "bien viaje."

The U.S. embargo successfully oppresses a proud people. When Pilar took us on a tour of the Old City, she talked of the revolution and said she is proud to be a Cuban. As I have mentioned earlier, citizens of Cuba are paid a pittance per month. Food is scarce in the market. Jobs are shared so everyone can work. The crime rate is low, illegal drug use is limited, the mentally ill and elderly are provided for, there are few homeless and people love Castro. Pilar said people love him because he loves the people and cares for the weakest, especially children. So what are we (the U.S. government) doing to Cubans? Is it really the threat of Communism or are we being mean-spirited and spiteful because Castro does not allow the U.S. to control the resources of the region? That is what Pilar told me is the U.S. motive behind the embargo.

We returned home to what we already knew: that Gleevec was an important medicine for Claudia to have. Lois Crilly became the only bright spot in the search for it. I met Lois a couple weeks before I moved to El Salvador. She is a Des Moines native and at the time I met her, she was a vice-president for Wellmark Blue Cross Blue Shield Dental of Iowa. Lois's generous heart has provided many resources to finance issues of peace and justice, and I was lucky to have benefited from her generosity. Lois dedicated herself to her profession so never married. She was childless and seemed to be a perfect match to join Claudia's battle for the cure of leukemia. I called Lois and explained Claudia's situation and our search for a bone marrow transplant or the cost of Gleevec. Lois joined the search and it was her long-term patience and professional knowledge of the medical field that became the energy for success in Claudia's cure of leukemia.

Lois established a fund for special expenses and it was from that money that we were able to purchase the first month of Gleevec for Claudia. But at the rate of $2,650, those funds would soon run out. So I turned to Dr. Boxer, the single response I had gotten when Tom Carney sent the request for a bone marrow transplant to his list of email addresses. I sent Dr. Boxer an email asking if he knew of any possible resources to pay for Gleevec for Claudia. He responded that Max Foundation would be that source, but they had already turned Dr. Valencia's solicitation down, which I relayed in a second communication to Dr. Boxer. A few days later he responded that a woman named Michelle would be contacting me. She did, and after telling me she was the person in charge with helping people from Latin America with the need Claudia had, I put her in touch with Dr. Valencia. The upshot of it all is Dr. Valencia began to receive Gleevec for over sixty of his patients with leukemia.

I began to think of Lois as Claudia's angel of mercy. When it was sure Claudia would receive Gleevec for life, Lois made contact with the University of Iowa Hospitals in Iowa City to establish a source of knowledge about Gleevec, its affects, and testing for results. The cancer department agreed to become a source for testing Claudia's progress by receiving samples of her blood on a quarterly basis. They also agreed to see Claudia in person once a year for a physical checkup and analysis of her progress. Though U.S. visas for Salvadorans are as scarce as robin's eggs in winter, Lois was able to secure a medical visa for Claudia so she could make that annual trip for a medical checkup at the University of Iowa Hospitals. It was a roller coaster ride, but on her last physical check up in the fall of 2008, Claudia was declared cured of her leukemia. And with that Claudia and her husband, Sergio, did what they had wanted to do for many years. They had a baby girl. Her name is Nadina, named after her mother, Claudia Nadina. Claudia resumed taking Gleevec after giving birth and likely will have to take it for many years to come. But it was music to hear she is cured, and that through this process I acquired one more Salvadoran daughter who calls me Papa. I think it not presumptuous that Nadina will call me Abuelo. And Lois Crilly is proud to be called Mama by her Salvadoran daughter, Claudia. And undoubtedly, she will be called Abuela by Nadina. I call her Angel of Miracles.

Chapter 12

The Beginning of Our Sister Parish Mission

Unless a grain of wheat falls to the ground, and dies, it remains alone. But if it dies, it will bear much fruit.
John 12.24

When I approached the Coordinating Council of Des Moines Presbytery in early 1999 with a request to do ministry in El Salvador, they were generous in their response. Although they were clear they had no money in the budget to pay me, they did suggest I be "commissioned" in a service before I go. I felt affirmed by the response. I had no problem with the idea of raising my own resources for living.

In September, 2001, there was a commissioning service was at Park Avenue Presbyterian Church in Des Moines. My new life as "Des Moines Presbytery's Designated Missionary to El Salvador" was launched. A sub-committee was formed by the Social Ministries Task Force of Presbytery to provide a communication and support base for my life. It adopted the name "Compañeros" and continues more than a decade later to function as the "state-side" base of support for what has become known as Our Sister Parish Mission.

I arrived in Berlin on October 23, 2001, to take up residency. I had envisioned living in the Parish Christian Education Wing, where I had lived for a year in 1994-1995. But there had been a falling-out between the parish team and the new priest. He considered them to be radical FMLN supporters with a leftist social orientation. They ultimately were asked to leave the church as their base of operation. FUNDAVIDA, a human rights organization which the parish team had helped organize a few years before, occupied a house with more space than they could use. It was a very comfortable home that a local doctor had constructed for himself and his family, but which they no longer occupied. Half of the three-bedroom, two-bath home became the home for the parish team.

So I arrived to a comfortable home with a touch of the First World. A soft landing for this gringo. The human rights organization that shared the house occupied the living room, a bedroom and a bathroom. Together we occupied the house. The doctor had it constructed, but his children felt more comfortable living in the city, so they abandoned it for the more cultured and socially acceptable possibilities of San Salvador. The doctor relented to his children's wishes and would drive to Berlin from San Salvador weekly to provide health care and slept in an apartment, returning to the city on weekends to be with his family. He is a good man and loves his patients. The people of Berlin are lucky to have decent health care, though his office lacks modern technology. The main entrance to the house was through a two-car garage and it had a nice sized backyard with two large avocado trees, surrounded by a high security wall completing the property.

I was glad to have the comforts of a house built for a doctor's family. But it was not that rather well appointed living space that made my move to this rustic setting seem predestined. It was the poor housing that surrounded the Casa Pastoral (pastoral team house) that were far less comfortable that the one I lived in; and the dirt floor huts with dirt for a front yard, that covered the mountainside below Berlin, in the cantónes, that drew me with a particular single-mindedness to live in that place. It increasingly brought back to my mind's surface the memories of my own childhood home near Dexter, Iowa that created this tug of embracing the needs of Salvadoran people. Just like in the cantónes of Berlin, there was no lush grass at my front door, so typical of Iowa's front yards. Had I been older at the time, I am sure I would have been embarrassed by the poverty that my home represented; but soon after the experience of violent trauma of my youth, we moved to a home that bore no indicators of the economic status we lived. The fear and sadness of my first six years of life were left behind like debris of a violent wind.

Years later when my spirit found its way into the soul of Salvadoran people, the violent winds of memory came back and laid the debris at my feet to help me remember my roots. Those roots moved me to instinctively understand the fight of nature's elements, which made the house cold and damp from the broken windows, no insulation, and missing siding that said out loud, "This is the home of a poor family." In the eleven years from my first visit to El Salvador, where I spent sixteen days in the Cantón El Tablón, until my arrival in 2001, I remembered my childhood, where I first became aware of what it meant to be poor and afraid. And the promise to no one in particular and everyone in general at a very young age that if ever I could do anything about it, I would.

I did not know much about matters of God and faith at that time in my childhood, but even now I can see the first inklings of spiritual insight that were sown in that promise. The promise I had made so long ago, I now understood to be a promise I was making to God, in all the naiveté yet richness of a child's faith. Down the mountainside from Berlin was the root of life I had lived in my childhood. Poverty housing and dirt for a lawn were calling me. I had come home to fulfill the promise I made decades ago that I would, in my life, work with whatever I had to work with, to do something about poverty. As I stood there in the backyard of what would become the Casa Pastoral, under the shade of a tall avocado tree, I sensed a stirring in my spirit and God's still small voice through the rustle of leaves above, that which Isaiah expressed long ago in a different time and space, *"here am I, send me."*

Chapter 13

The Seed Grows
First Projects and Growth in Mission

So many say, "What can one person do? What is the sense of our small effort?" they cannot see that we must lay one brick at a time, take one step at a time; we can only be responsible for the one action of the present moment. But we can beg for an increase of love in our hearts that will vitalize our individual actions, and know that God will take them, and multiply them just as Jesus multiplied the loaves and fishes.
Dorothy Day

Every delegation I took to visit El Tablón had the same question: What do the people need that we can take for them? By the time the parish team sent me a communication through the SHARE Foundation that they would like to meet me, there had been four visits by gringos to the cantón. Each time the residents received generous gifts of clothing, education supplies, and money. The purpose of the parish team's invitation was to invite me to come live among them in order to get to know the people of the land and the culture that guides their lives. Their invitation grew out of their hope that, in order for me to continue a relationship with the poor of their land, I had to understand the dynamics I was creating with the gifts that were given by those well-intentioned gringos. It was a persistent realty that they knew the delegations and their gifts could not last forever, just long enough to cause the poor communities to become dependent. They had seen them come and go from other countries before. The gifts were a Band-Aid on the gash of poverty and, while well-intentioned, created the sort of dependency that stifled the community's long-term sustainable development.

That year I lived in the education wing of the church was an immersion into Salvadoran life and culture in the Berlin municipality. Gently, the people I came to know and love returned the favor by taking my life out of the context of the foreign invaders who, over the centuries, by creating dependencies, removed from these people any real sense of their community pride, their power and their wealth; leaving them a jobless, poorly educated, industry-less, poverty-stricken people. Besides the historic human damage done in the name of Christ by the Spanish Inquisition, which in ways still lingers, more recently they had fought a civil war to regain the power of political will for the people, so they could decide their future for their nation. They did not, and do not, need any other nation, institution or person, becoming the authority and power over their social and political development. Their most recent experience with the U. S., the land of the free, funding, sustaining, and arming their oppressors, was proof enough of this. Their future and hopes for human and social development needed to depend on their own leadership, their own exertion of power and their own economic development. It is an act of ill will and, in fact, is the portrayal of the image of the ugly American, to make the rules and exert influence and authority over the development process. I had learned about third world poverty. Now it was time to learn how to be supportive, but not authoritative, in the country's efforts to seek solutions to widespread poverty.

So in 1994 I began to listen and I learned about the people and their lives. Even though they are appreciative of that handout that staves off hunger, they do not want to become a welfare society, living off the dole of the First World. I listened to the history of their oppression, the deeply rooted fear caused by death squad threats and murders; I heard of their hopes for a brighter future, if not for themselves, at least for their children; and embraced a sense of the pride they possess when they organized together and become a unified voice able to demand the programs that they would need that would build their dreams.

I listened to these people as they spoke of their dreams of education, medical care, and employment that would provide a modicum of an income to sustain their basic needs. As I listened to them, some of whom have become life-long friends, it was my growing awareness of their culture of hope that caused my love for them to grow within to a point that it seemed to nearly burst the seams of my heart. My year of immersion in El Salvador built a bridge between south and north to allow and encourage visitors, not invaders, to be cheer leaders in support of their quest for social and political development. It was through that year of engagement that I learned that any role in which I might be privileged to serve, it could never, never, be a role that assumed any decision-making in the process of development.

The parish team, in that year that I became acclimated to Salvadoran culture and life, taught me that controlling behavior and the foreign--assumed superior--influence has potential to turn their faith journey into a capitalist project that cannot survive in the poverty of developing nations like El Salvador. For a foreigner to assume such importance in the process is not only capable of crushing their dreams, but also it is simply and grossly unjust. It is an act contrary to the oft-touted understanding within the Church of the "Self Development of People." The voices on that parish team, as well as many, many friends who lived on the mountainside, taught me that the time-worn slogan of "pulling yourself up by the bootstraps," promoting individualism and personal accumulation of wealth is not healthy in a culture that possesses limited resources that must be shared, not exploited. They believed so strongly in the will of the people for the good of the masses, that they refused to take a salary, or receive any compensation, for their work. Sadly, that would in time change, caused by the growth of the parish team into an institution in which profits and expenses were a priority consideration over issues of justice. Foreign authority was again allowed to creep back into the decision making process, which came about, in part, through a jealousy that took root in the midst of the team members. As I reflect, I am grateful that it I was not a witness to it, nor did it happen under my tenure as Des Moines Presbytery's Designated Missionary to El Salvador.

It was the authority of the Salvadoran leadership that drove program development for Our Sister Parish Mission (OSPM). It was social concern for the good of the masses, not just a few, that drove the philosophy of mission development. Always, it was the parish team of Berlin who decided the outcome of the "who," "what," "where," "when," and "why" questions. When I arrived in Berlin to live at the parish team house, I was given status as a member on the team, not as an officer or official gringo, influential American funder.

Bob Cook with Parish Team of Casa Pastoral, March 2005

Never did I assume a position of leadership or decision-making in the six years I served as the Presbytery's missionary to El Salvador. Up to 2001 it was the Parish priest who was the rudder for mission direction. That was to destined to change abruptly with the appointment of Fr. Silvio by the Franciscan Order, which had its headquarters in Guatemala. Today, I am convinced that the Order's Leadership in Guatemala had no idea of the turmoil that one of their number would come to create, at the Parish of Berlin, in the story that follows.

The focus of Fr. Silvio's resistance to the parish team was toward one of its members, Milagro Rodriquez. She is an intelligent, savvy, and strong-willed woman, who had served in the capacity of social change agent for the parish since the end of the war in 1992. Everyone from the north, who visited the Casa Pastoral, adored Milagro for her wit, charm, beauty and powerful presence. She had grown up on a coffee plantation in Cantón San Filipe, where her father worked long hours for meager wages. She lived the oppression that drove the revolution, and it was that experience that made her a fireball of justice for her people. She cherished the people as and for who they are; but it was her passion for justice and her force of will, in regard to the needs of the poor, which became the shibboleth of jealous discontent for some who worked close to her.

At the top of the list of her openly avowed enemies was Fr. Silvio. I am still not clear as to why he became such a virulent opponent, whether it was his desire to possess her power without having earned it, or a conservative approach to his faith that thought women should only serve in certain ways, or politics alone. He disliked her profoundly, and he was a chauvinist who felt threatened by her. His solution, as to her leadership, to simply rid himself of this female canker took the form of an ultimatum to the entire parish team to change their "radical philosophical approach" to the work of their social programs, or change their place of work altogether. The parish team composed at the time of Milagro, Balmore, Blanca, and Jesus were not about to be bullied by Silvio and his "my way or the highway" approach, and so, the next chapter of OSPM began to take shape with a new location for their work.

Originally, it was Fr. Silvio who issued me a letter of invitation (though it was Milagro who typed it) to live at the parish of Berlin. When I arrived on October 23 to take up residence, my first official act was a meeting with Silvio. He made no ultimatums with me, although it was clear from his explanation of the parish team's presumed errant ways, that I had the choice of working with him or not work at all in the parish of St. Joseph. My own questions to him about my role made it clear I would be a fundraising source for remodeling of a century-old church, with the further objective of expanding it and razing the old support pillars that obstructed the worshippers' view of the altar. That was his primary goal. I told him I would let him know later of my decision, and that I had no interest in returning to Iowa at that time.

After conferring with the parish team about the matter, it was their opinion that I did not have to worry about Silvio's expectations. I could work with them as a member of the parish team, for they were now working under the authority of the bishop, not that of Silvio. A phone call to him confirmed his agreement. I could work with the parish team, but he would also like to meet me in the near future. I communicated to Silvio my decision to remain in Berlin and to serve with the parish team by authority of the bishop. We parted without the customary handshake, and I never had another conversation with Silvio in the entire five years he was parish priest. The bishop not only gave me permission to labor with the team, but he also provided me with a lay missionary card with signature and seal of the diocese.

The eviction of the parish team from the education wing had taken place before my return in 2001. As noted in the previous chapter, it was easily remedied with the invitation by a human rights organization, FUNDAVIDA to share office space. A year later, the FUNDAVIDA office moved to a different location, and the team became the sole occupant of what is now known as the Casa Pastoral (Pastoral Team House), located at Av. 14 de Diciembre, Barrio La Parroquia, Berlin. And so, Milagro, Blanca, Balmore, and Jesus became responsible for administration of the program and an office. Doing so was in an area of personal development, project organizing, and financial accountability, in which none of them had ever been trained. However, with hopeful hearts, they left behind the first-class partnership that had existed for the decade of the 1990s with the parish priest and, became a first-class act of social development in the cantónes of the parish of St. Joseph on the mountainside in eastern El Salvador. Two years later, with the help of a loan and a grant from Sister Ana from Spain, who is a good friend of Milagro's, the parish team purchased the house that was their office. Sister Ana came from a religious order in Spain to live at the Berlin parish in the early 1990s, and was the setting out of which their friendship developed. With property ownership as a factor in the growth of the team, the decision was made to become El Salvador's version of a private non-profit, and the team members, including myself, became owners of the property. Today, according to the laws of the country, I am a 1/6 land baron in El Salvador.

The early years of program development, although not planned development, were important groundwork for what was to come in the first decade of the 21st century. That development included: .

- A school for grades one through six in El Tablón was reopened, after the signing of the peace accords in 1992. The people of the community did the labor to replace the roof and remove dirt that had been washed into the classrooms by heavy rains over the years. A gift of $8,000was provided by Des Moines Presbytery to make the repairs possible.

- Des Moines Presbytery continued to provide 50 percent of the annual Rural Harvest Hunger Offering for agricultural assistance to the farmers on the mountainside. It was a significant gift that helped provide food to people who often lacked sufficient beans and corn to stifle their family's hunger.

- After the first official Des Moines Presbytery delegation traveled to Berlin in 1993, a movement grew out of efforts of Rev. James Ray and Rev. Joyce Bassler to raise $2,000 that was donated by Presbyterian Women groups of Des Moines Presbytery to teach six women in the Cantón El Tablón how to sew. After six months of training the women received treadle sewing machines, donated by families in central Iowa, and transported to Berlin by a Pastors' for Peace Caravan, organized by Catholic Peace Ministries of Des Moines. It was the creative thinking of Carmen and Don Hampton from Trinity Presbyterian Church in Indianola, Iowa, who provided maintenance to extend the life of those machines, in a very dirty and less than ideal environment. They learned how to clean and repair pedal sewing machines and then, using their own financial resources, journeyed to El Tablón to renew the machines.

- Chapter 6 included the story of Rev. Bill Calhoun and the delegation from his church from Newton First Presbyterian. That delegation was the forerunner to the medical delegations that have since 1998 provided medical exams to the poor on the mountainside. It is more than symbolic that the referred to delegation in 1997 assisted in cost and labor to construct an adobe clinic in the Cantón Virginia, a neighboring Cantón to El Tablón.

The very able Salvadoran leadership on the parish team grew as a thorn in the side of Fr. Silvio. During the entire five years of his tenure as the parish priest, he referred to the Casa Pastoral as the Casa Protestante (protestant house, because of my Protestant roots) and in every way possible put the work of the team in a negative light. But the success of the projects mentioned above gave momentum for the mission, and hope rose in the eyes of the people on the mountainside. However, as any learned sociologist would surmise, it was obvious that growing pains would come soon to the parish team.

In May, 1999, I visited Berlin for a month, along with Kent Newman, who had knowledge to share with those interested about solar power to use for cooking, and Tammy Less, who, with her husband Ron, had given a sizable donation with the condition she travel there to see the work being done. The day we left Berlin to come home, the priest called me to his office for a chat. The purpose was to propose to me that a church be constructed in the Cantón El Tablón. Hopes rose in the hearts of the people on the mountainside of Berlin, as rumors spread of a soon to be built church building of their own.

The Catholic Church had done a good job of organizing its numbers in the wake of the Council of Medelin of 1968. At the Council's direction areas like Berlin that lacked sufficient priests made a decision to train and organized Delegates of the Word, who would be religious leadership in each of the cantónes It was a very good plan, for besides the church having a communicator between the cantón and the priests of the parish, it also brought the church to the elderly and infirm who could not make the arduous walk to Sunday Mass in Berlin. So news of the construction of a church in El Tablón brought more hope to people of faith that a project was being planned to make the church present to the poorest of the poor.

An architect was contacted by the priest and he was instructed to draw plans for a new church, but the father provided no criteria for the architect to follow for the project. The architect began with the assumption that wealthy gringos were paying the bill and resources were, therefore, unlimited. The plans he drew reflected that belief with a construction cost of just under $100,000. This became the first of several hurdles, which would slow the project to a crawl over the next several years.

But for the leadership of Rev. Mark Davis, pastor at Heartland Presbyterian Church in Clive, Iowa, the church project in El Tablón might have never been constructed. The Heartland congregation had become the first of Des Moines area churches to commit to the mission design of OSPM, which was to establish a relationship with a cantón on the Berlin Mountain. Heartland's cantón was El Tablón. I had watched Mark grow Heartland Presbyterian Church in Clive from its initial stages of new church development into a dynamic ministry on the western edge of Des Moines. I knew him to be a person with great organizing, pastoral, and administrative skills. He is intelligent, rational, a wonderful singer, plays several musical instruments, preaches excellent sermons, and is a man of deep and true faith. In my mind, if anyone could provide leadership to construct the church in El Tablón, Mark could.

I called Mark and asked to have lunch with him. I sat across from him at a bagel cafe near his church, and I wasted little time asking if he would consider adding to his successful ministry a mission in El Salvador. I reviewed with him the situation of the Berlin Parish, specifically El Tablón. Heartland already knew some of the people in Berlin, including Haydee and Milagro, mother and daughter. One of the first medical delegations from Newton had made arrangements for them to journey to Des Moines for Milagro to have corrective foot surgery. Dr. Jeffrey Farber provided the surgical skills, Blank Children's Hospital provided for her recovery. And it was Joyce and Jim Hoffman, members of Heartland, who provided hospitality for three months while Milagro recovered from the surgery. An additional person of importance I want to mention is Bill Fischer, a member of Heartland. He had already visited Berlin and El Tablón with a delegation I took there in 1999. (After more than 20 visits over the years, Bill felt called to retire from his executive position with Xerox to organize ESNA Village Network to do development work in El Salvador). Several other Heartland members became known persons in Berlin. The many broken hearts caused by the poverty they had witnessed embraced the vision of the mission. Mark agreed to take the possibility of a cantón/church relationship to the church for a vote.

A logical next step was for a delegation to visit Berlin. A small delegation from Heartland made the trip to El Salvador and meet with the parish team and the directiva (city council) of El Tablón. Upon returning, the delegation recommended to the Heartland congregation that they make a five-year commitment to a relationship with El Tablón. The relationship was approved by unanimous vote.

Tomás Ventura was the Delegate of the Word for the Cantón El Tablón. He had become a member of the parish team by 2001, and he had become a good friend of mine and many from Heartland from the several visits I made to El Tablón. He was instrumental in helping the team redesign a plan for the church of more reasonable cost, that took the shape of a community kitchen, sewing house, clinic, and bathrooms complete with septic tank.

Space for a church was included in the design but would be a future construction. Land next to Tomás' home was purchased as the location of the project and hopes ran high by the time I arrived to join the Parish Team in 2001 that construction would begin soon. But because of disagreement between Tomás and the rest of the members on the parish team, construction did not begin for at least another year. It was the policy of the team that residents of the cantón to receive a development project, would provide labor for it, guided by a paid foreman. Tomás had visited the U.S., and was firmly entrenched of the belief that the wealth he had seen was so great, that it was only just that the unemployed residents of his church be provided jobs. Negotiations became heated arguments, which in turn brought Tomás' resignation from the parish team, and soon he was carrying water for Fr. Silvio, who seemingly took great delight in the potential, utter failure of the project.

Looking back on the situation, it is obvious that Tomás' pride and position of influence in the community was on the line. He had promised members of his church they would not have to donate their labor but rather they would have paying jobs on the project. Thus he began communication directly with Heartland Church, whom he believed to be his good friends, and whom he also believed he could easily persuade into taking his side in the dispute in employing his church members to build the project. But Mark, and Heartland church's leadership, had understood from the beginning that the Parish team was the authority and organizing body for all construction issues and decisions. The Tomás/Silvio alliance created a barrier of resistance to the parish team's attempt to do ministry on the mountainside. It brought development of the many positive projects in El Tablón to a complete standstill.

Tomás' friendship with Silvio added a serious dynamic for the parish team. When Silvio declared the parish team house to be a "Protestant House," Tomás was in agreement. The declaration became a threat for many of the residents on the mountainside. The insinuation was that anyone who visited the Casa Protestante had chosen sides, which put their Catholic membership in question. It was no surprise that the members of the El Tablón church, Tomás' church, joined the chorus of protest, bent on destroying the work of the parish team. Their influence spread to other cantónes, and visitors to the parish team house from cantónes became fewer in number.

Tension increased also because even if residents in the cantóns disagreed with Silvio, it was no small thing to act contrary to the wishes of the local priest. I give credit to a committed and strong-spirited parish team that would, with time and patience, give OSPM credibility. With that credibility came support from some residents of the cantónes in spite of Silvio's negative influence.

A cultural lesson from the relationship problems that surfaced in the development of this project is we, the gringos, cannot be mediators between the parties. I asked in a parish team meeting at the height of the growing problems what I could do to help reconcile Tomás and the team (I felt Fr. Silvio was not worth the effort it would take, nor did I think the devil felt my soul was worth enough). They said I should not become a voice for or against one side or the other, that it would reduce my effectiveness as a friend of the community. Also, there was no way I would have knowledge of all the dynamics involved in problem between the parties. But anything I could do or say to minimize contact between

Tomas and the Heartland delegations would be helpful. I tried, but Heartland's love for Tomas and his people was not diminished by delay of the project, and it became next to impossible to prevent personal and social conversations between them. Nevertheless, it is important to remember to not become a voice to lead as well as not to criticize even the "enemy."

What is it that carries a mission without a plan, like OSPM, to keep moving forward and to maintain a sense of integrity, even in the face of adversity and criticism by the power of an institution, or an autocrat, like that demonstrated by Silvio? A piece of that answer lies in the history of its integrity to care for the people. If there is a number one need that is the common thread among the people, it is water. Potable water that does not come from contaminated rivers and springs. The Parish Team knew that, and began a coalition effort between themselves, CIS (Center for International Solidarity) in San Salvador, and Agua Viva that drilled wells for the cantónes of the country. They made one attempt at a well that was dry before my arrival. Two more were tried after my arrival. One was a dry hole and the other resulted in a trapped drill caused by an earthquake. It was a $12,000 drill and the loss was the demise of the well-drilling endeavor. A hydrologist later determined that the water table for the area had been significantly lowered by the January 13 and February 13, 2001, earthquakes; which confirmed the effort of drilling wells to be fruitless and should be abandoned. However, the endeavor did serve to establish considerable respect for the intentions of the team in the cantónes.

With the failure to find water, and construction of the El Tablón community center project at a standstill, meetings at the Casa Pastoral diminished and activity was infrequent. Then, like Pentecost, the Spirit of the Living God fell afresh on the land and new life took shape for the mission. I had been selected by the Des Moines Catholic Peace Ministry Board to receive the coveted 2002 Maurice Dingman Peace Award. When I was in Des Moines to receive it, I took the opportunity to preach at a couple churches, one of them being First Presbyterian Church of Des Moines.

I told about the mission's progress in El Salvador and included information about a wished-for water project by the Cantón San Felipe

Arriba. I had learned in a meeting with the leadership of the cantón that they had for years wished for a rain water collection system to serve as a water source in the six month dry season. USAID had committed the cost of materials and labor for the project, but their condition for such a donation was that the community had to own the land on which the project was constructed. The $7000 necessary for the cost of the land was out of reach for anyone in the cantón. So the project languished for lack of land ownership.

It was a rather small gathering that day for worship at First Presbyterian Church of Des Moines. It was a lesson for me not to discount support just because of small numbers of people. After the worship ended an elderly gentleman approached me and suggested the church should be able to pay the $7,000 cost for the land. A meeting was quickly organized and it was unanimous that the money be provided from the church's endowment. I returned to Berlin with $7,000 in the bank for the project and the second cantón sister parish relationship was established between San Felipe Arriba and First Presbyterian Church of Des Moines. I witnessed hope rising again in the eyes of the people and credibility for the team gained footing again on the mountainside when people heard news about the water collection tank.

At the same time, Heartland continued to insist the parish team was the organizing body for all projects, and an agreement was reached between the team and the Directiva of El Tablón for construction of the community center to begin. Recognizing the need for nourishment in the families of El Tablón, an agreement was reached that those who helped construct the center would be paid with food at the end of each work week. It was an acceptable negotiation among all parties involved. Donations of food were given to workers in recognition of donations of labor for the project being constructed in the cantón. Critical nutritional needs were met while at the same time, labor was donated for the project under construction.

Soon after the water tank project was finished in San Felipe Arriba, church/cantón relationships grew in number. I do not have the dates of their commitment, but within two years the following churches had agreed to form a cantón/church relationship to grow OSPM into a project of considerable size and purpose. They include:

- Heartland Presbyterian Church of Clive with El Tablón. The projects include a community center with a community kitchen, sewing house with solar panels to provide electricity, a clinic and a community kitchen. Since my retirement an elementary school was constructed in Tablón Serna which provides education for the early grades. It was common for children to be left out of education because of the long walk to the far end of the cantón where the school is located. Before having to walk the two kilometers to the main school for upper grade education. Heartland also paid for a high school teacher so the youth of the cantón could attain ninth grade, which is required to attend high school in Berlin.

- Ankeny Presbyterian Church with Cantón Corozal. Ankeny paid the cost of constructing a mountain spring water collection tank for the cantón to have potable water. The water from the spring is pure. The church has also provided fertilizer to individual farmers at planting time to increase yield and thus provide additional source of nutrition for the cantón families. Since my retirement a community center is in process of being planned.

- Dallas Center Presbyterian Church with Cantón Virginia. Projects paid for by Dallas Center include the construction of a church that was destroyed in the 2001 earthquake and the construction of a water tank and community kitchen next to the church. Fertilizer was provided for farmers at planting time to increase yield.

- Westminster Presbyterian with Cantón San Francisco. The first project undertaken by Westminster was to install solar panels on eighty-one homes in the cantón to provide electricity to operate small appliances and provide light to see by in the dark of night. Since my retirement, a new church has been constructed and dedicated.

- Trinity Presbyterian Church of Indianola with Casero Casa de Zinc. Trinity paid the cost of a fence to surround the water collection tanks of the small community. They also provided fertilizer for the farmers at planting season.

- Newton First Presbyterian Church with Cantón Munosis. The cantón was historically considered to be a caserio (group of homes) of El Tablón. But it organized its own directiva and expressed interest in a relationship. First Presbyterian Church of Newton had initiated medical delegation and then joined forces with Sacred Heart Catholic Church to provide medical exams on a yearly basis. The Presbyterian Church in recent years opted to add a cantón/church relationship to its commitment. That has taken place since my retirement and I do not have information about the projects it has initiated.

The mission attained ecumenical status with the addition of a Catholic and a Christian Church commitment. They include:

- St. Boniface Catholic Parish with Cantón El Recreo. St. Boniface assisted with the purchase of land for a soccer field on which will be constructed a community center and a playground for children. Fertilizer was provided to small farmers at planting season to increase yield. Since my retirement, a church was constructed and dedicated to replace the adobe one that was partially destroyed in the 1984 earthquake. In addition, a community museum has been opened.

- Wakonda Christian Church with Cantón Las Delicias. The church paid the cost of construction of a water collection tank, using the roof of the church as the collection roof. The church also paid the cost of smaller water tanks for families to collect their own rainwater during the rainy season.

Members of the St. Boniface Church delegation
Photo by Michael J. Arkwright

One other church/cantón relationship was attempted, but never could be completed, because of land ownership questions. Kilduff and Reasoner United Methodist Churches, under the leadership of Rev. Duane Skidmore, had responded to Cantón Colon's request for assistance in repair of an existing rain water collection tank. It was an open tank made of boulders and cement that had been constructed around the turn of the twentieth century. It was at least five meters deep and fifteen meters across. A large, slightly elevated piece of land served as a rain collection area that drained water into a large tube that emptied into the tank. A broken drain in the bottom of the tank had originally served as a source of water for livestock tanks by draining water from the tank to livestock watering tanks that were located further down the hill. New plans called for a covering over the tank, repair of the drain and purchase of the land on which the tank was set. Kilduff and Reasoner United Methodist Churches had sent $6000 for the project, which allowed the Team to hire an attorney to begin land ownership transfer to the cantón.

I will never forget the meeting with a man who thought he and his brothers were the owners of the land. The attorney's information was that in fact they were not the owners. And there were a number of legal maneuvers it would take to straighten out the land ownership question. Each successive meeting exposed more problems than solutions. A year became two, two became three and there was no end in sight. Being a gringo from a country where land ownership is a relatively simple thing, I inquired how much more time was needed to figure out ownership. No one knew. Like a mire of, the legal process bogged down any headway on the land ownership question. That in turn effectively ended any interest in the project. The money was returned to the churches minus several hundred that paid the attorney's fees for doing who knows what. To this day, the large open tank serves to provide polluted rain-water to those brave enough to stand on the edge to dip water with a bucket tied to a rope. I say brave, for if they fell into the tank there is no ladder on which to exit, and one may drown before a rescue could be made.

The Silvio/Tomás vitriolic diatribe continued against the parish team and their work was relentless in spite of the obvious good work being done on the mountainside. Silvio spoke particularly harshly about Milagro, and I always assumed he was most upset by her strong, charismatic personality that kept him from winning everyone over to his side. It was a particularly difficult situation for visiting delegations to understand. I was caught in the middle, having been asked by the parish team to minimize as much as I could the development of Tomás' relationship with visiting delegation members. It was a particularly difficult and sometimes embarrassing task to try to interrupt a friendship for no good apparent reason, at least from a gringo point of view.

It was difficult for gringos to see the harsh reality of the relationships between Silvio and Tomás on the one hand and the parish team on the other. Often members of visiting delegations would suggest that with a reconciling counselor, perhaps friendships could develop out of a "bad history of misunderstandings." Predictably, two people from a delegation took it upon themselves to meet with Silvio to begin what they assumed would be the first stages of that reconciling process. Silvio, predictably, spoke badly of Milagro and said she did bad work. Inevitably word about the meeting got back to the parish team, along with the negative expressions that Silvio now had made to gringos. It was the straw that broke the camel's back. The parish team filed suit against Silvio for slander. I want to tell you here and now that no matter how a community might feel about the priest, no matter how badly he has spoken about the people, nothing the priest has said or done short of sexual misconduct warrants, in the eyes of the community, a lawsuit. As news of the suit spread, tensions mounted. For the first time before and since the lawsuit, I felt a sense of intimidation while walking the street alone. A stone the size of a baseball whizzed past my head from an unknown person in a crowd on the street corner. I didn't tell the parish team, but I stayed home for a few weeks until after the suit was settled.

The day for trial arrived. Silvio strolled in with a counterfeit laugh and an attitude of irritating nonchalance, as if to say, "What is it that such people as this should waste my time?" Tomás was included in the suit and his entire church of forty-some people came in a caravan. It was an unsettling moment, and for the first time I thought about leaving Berlin and not looking back. But during the trial some of the people from El Tablón , some I had known for years since my first visit in 1990 caught my eye and shrugged, as though to say, "I am sorry." The trial lasted about two hours. While the judge did not find Silvio guilty, he did say Silvio should cease and desist from negative comments about the parish team. And to the parish team, he said, "Let it go." It calmed the community and no mention was made of it again, at least not to me. Silvio stayed on another year but the turmoil he had caused up to then did cease. The parish team did not get the ruling they wanted, but it was a more peaceful time from then on. And it seemed the delegations were more understanding that it was not just a "relationship problem" between the parties involved, but rather a serious problem that had interfered with the work of the team up to that point.

A sister cantón relationship was not a requirement to participate with OSPM. A group from five churches in the Marshalltown area made a trip to Berlin to check it out and see what options there might be for mission. John Calvin and Immanuel Presbyterian Churches in Milwaukee provided several thousand dollars a year for a few years for purchase of fertilizer for farmers. The parish of First Presbyterian Church of Dexter and Pitzer Presbyterian Church provided finances to fund a project that corrected a drainage problem that allowed sewage from the local slaughterhouse to flood into homes in one part of Berlin.

Two groups with which I continue to be involved after retirement are student delegations from Drake University, organized by St. Catherine of Siena Parish near Drake and the University of Iowa organized and led by Rev. Marsha Acord, who is a chaplain with the Wesley Foundation. They contract with me to provide on the ground leadership for their time in El Salvador. Neither of the student delegations have specific ties with Berlin. The Drake delegation has an unofficial relationship with the Cantón Conacaste. It is the cantón where Reyna Sandoval, the woman who ran in front of my car, lived with her two children. And it is where the St. Catherine Parish established a sister relationship in construction of a new church for that community. The Drake student delegation is unique in that regard.

The University of Iowa student delegation also has a unique focus for their annual trip to El Salvador. They pay the university costs for Erikc Hernesto Martinez Mindez, a young person who grew up in Berlin and now attends the University in San Miguel. My relationship with Erikc grew out of a $10 loan which he failed to repay. Voluntarily. Erikc calls me Papa. I tell the story of our relationship in Chapter XIIII, which describes my relationship with six families I have unofficially adopted as a result of my life in El Salvador.

I was a man with a vision, not a man with a plan. One day in 2006, I looked at OSPM and realized vision had produced a mission that needed an administrator and long-term planning. Administration is not my long suit, and it was then that I believed I should take an early retirement, so a person with adequate organizing skills could become missionary to the project. It took awhile, but Compañeros has hired Kathy Mahler to administer OSPM. I love El Salvador, the beauty of the land and the kindness of its people. So I thought, why not retire there? I located a very nice three-bedroom home with vaulted ceilings, marble tile floors, a maid's quarters (which I would never have used), a cistern that guaranteed water 24/7, and a patio that overlooked a huge garden of fruit trees and flowering plants for rent. It was up the mountain from San Salvador at Kilometer seven on the way to Planes de Rendero. It was a short distance to enjoy the night-lights of the city. So I rented the house that was too luxurious, too large, too comfortable, and with the option to buy, which I intended to do six months later.

I moved in the month of my retirement, August. At the end of September, I saw my first scorpion. It was a bit disconcerting that it was on the pillow next to mine. The next morning I was stung by one that had taken up residence in my bathrobe on the floor. They sting with a vengeance. Where there is one there is more, in my case many more. I killed as many as thirty. Two more stung me. So I called an exterminator and he assured me he could rid the house of the vermin. He sprayed in October. Scorpions remained. He sprayed in November. Scorpions remained.

On December 2, rather early in the morning, I prepared to drive down to the city to do some early Christmas shopping. As I walked up the two stairs from my sunken dining room to the living room I saw a snake slither under the front door. It was a colorful snake and I immediately recognized the markings as that of a coral snake, one that will kill within hours if bitten. I was petrified with fear and my screams brought a security man running, expecting to find who knows what. When I pointed to the snake he, with some nonchalance, perhaps more than was required from my point of view, pulled his machete from its place on his belt and severed the head of the snake from its body. With a smirk he walked away, certain that I was likely afraid of mice and my own shadow, too, and assured that his employment was forever secured with this gringo living in the villa.

The snake had a message for me. With clarity I saw the biblical expression of plagues of Egypt. God did not need to be so dramatic in his message to me that this house was luxury that went far beyond the simplicity of lifestyle I had chosen years before when I moved to El Salvador. I called the owners in Nicaragua and explained I no longer was interested in purchasing the home because of the plagues, first the scorpions and now the coral snake. Their surprise was not so much my decision to not purchase the home but rather that in the seven years they lived in the house they had never seen a scorpion let alone a coral snake. It made me wonder whether the security guard might be in cahoots with the vermin.

I had moved out by the end of December. I made my home with one of the families I had unofficially adopted, Carlos and Daniela and their three children. By the end of February, I was certain beyond a doubt that I was not interested in living with a family, especially one with three growing children. With nowhere else to go, I moved back to Des Moines. In April of 2007, I had an opportunity to be an interim pastor at Highland Park Presbyterian Church. At first I resisted, as I had a round-trip ticket to return to El Salvador in September. But after Cecilia, the cook at the Casa Pastoral, asked me in a telephone conversation, "What I was doing for God in Iowa?" Cooks as prophets, I didn't have a chance, so I relented and made a four-month commitment. In the end, my term with Highland Park Presbyterian Church lasted for two years, two months, and two days. As I write this, I have assumed a new interim position at Union Park Presbyterian Church in Des Moines. I am very happy serving them and am in no particular hurry for them to hurry and find my replacement.

Overall, I must say I am elated and fortunate to have had the experiences of life that I have had. God willing, the years I spend at Union Park Presbyterian Church will truly be my final days of work. But I have learned in life that I plan, God smiles, and makes His/Her own plan for what my life will be. Wherever God sends me, I only ask that it be free of scorpions or snakes, coral or otherwise.

Chapter 14

The Celebrations and Tears of Micro-business

"I believe that even our mistakes and errors are not in vain, and it is no harder for God to deal with them than what we regard as our good deeds, I believe that God is no timeless fate, that that God waits for and answers upright prayer and responsible deeds.
Dietrich Bonhoeffer

Erick Davidson is one of the smartest men I know. In addition, he is one of the best community organizers I know, having learned organizing techniques from the best, Joe Fagan and Hugh Espey, while working for Citizens for Community Improvement in Des Moines. His partner, and soon to be wife, Meredith is smart and a good organizer, but what she brought to the table was charisma and beauty. As a team, they formed the micro-business Don Justo Coffee for export from Berlin to Iowa. Erick was the brains and Meredith was the charm that made Don Justo Coffee a successful business. Today it belongs to the parish team with fifty cents per pound sold going to Compañeros administrative costs, and one dollar per pound going to the promoter of sales and an average of $2.50 per pound going into the parish team coffers. In a perfect world, Erick and Meredith would, in my opinion, be receiving monthly compensation from Don Justo coffee for their work organizing the business. But after the organizing was complete and sales were being made, a conflict rose over distribution of profits, which raised the larger question, *who owned the business?* Ultimately, the parish team asked Erick and Meredith to leave the project.

Don Justo Coffee

Local small coffee farm being paid for his coffee.

I confess, I made an assumption that could have prevented the ownership conflict had I involved Compañeros in the invitation to Erick and Meredith to be organizers for the coffee export business. I only reported to Compañeros that Erick and Meredith would be moving to Berlin for six months to be organizers of the coffee project. But there were never conversations between both parties. Had they met, it is likely those critical questions would have been raised and resolved from the beginning. But with unanswered, critical questions, there were set in motion two visions of the same project, which, in the end, nearly destroyed the project completely.

This is how it happened. A few days before I moved to El Salvador, I visited Erick and Meredith's home to say goodbye. They had purchased a large home behind the Catholic Worker Community in Des Moines. They bought it with the intention of remodeling it and selling it for a profit to provide living and education expenses when they moved to Ohio, where Erick planned to study for his doctorate degree. They were creative in their approach to life, so I took Erick seriously when he requested that I let them know if I found an opportunity for him and Meredith to organize a coffee export business in El Salvador. I had no doubt in their ability to do it and moreover it would be, I mused, a creative way to provide income for the mission.

In January, 2002, about three months after I moved to Berlin as missionary for Des Moines Presbytery, Stella Gonzales came to the Casa Pastoral with a gift and a challenge. The gift was twenty pounds of coffee. She explained that it had been grown on the family finca (plantation), on the other side of Santiago de Maria, and then transported to Berlin where they own a place to roast, grind, and package the coffee for sale. The finca had been in her husband Vidal's family for many decades and more recently he had, after three years of experimenting, created a flavorful, aromatic coffee from a blend of three varieties of beans. The challenge she gave me was to give it a taste test, to share it with gringo friends, and if we all felt it was quality coffee, to consider a coffee export business, which could be financially lucrative for everyone. When I made a return trip to Des Moines in February, I took with me the twenty pounds of coffee. My first "taste test" stop was at the home and Erick and Meredith. They, along with many other people who tried the coffee in the next two weeks declared it to be an excellent flavor. The vote was in, and it was a winner!

The exact timeline for what followed is somewhat fuzzy, but it took little time to see the fruit of Erick and Meredith's work. They had sold their house for a handsome profit and used some of the proceeds to pay their airfare to Berlin. They rented a small apartment above the hardware store and hit the ground running. The name Don Justo was agreed to for the product, named after Vidal's father whose name was Justo. I made regular reports to Compañeros about progress being made and when a logo for the coffee was needed, Sue Burns, a member of Compañeros, used her art skills to produce it. It was an act that showed the Compañeros' sense of ownership in the business. A price for what Stella and Vidal would receive for coffee was negotiated. Erick calculated a retail price for the coffee at $8 per pound. Analysis as a quality product by the public, they said, would require the coffee to be organic certified and free trade certified. They succeeded in the organic status but were denied Free Trade status because there was already a glut of free trade coffee titles on the market and the certifying office did not want to create more. It took several months to have everything in place and not once did Erick and Meredith ask to be reimbursed for living expenses, nor any other expense incurred by the organizing process.

Meredith became the coffee sales promoter. She made a couple of trips to Des Moines from El Salvador to meet with churches interested in selling coffee. She explained profits would go primarily to the parish team and she would receive a dollar per pound as coordinator of sales. Though I suggested several times that it was important to include a small amount of profit to the Compañeros, it fell on deaf ears. No mention was made for the Compañeros to receive my suggested fifty cents a pound. Sales began to increase and then topped off at seven hundred to one thousand pounds per month.

Erick carried the compassion he felt for the underdog to the small coffee farmers that surrounded Vidal and Stella's finca. The going rate paid for coffee at coffee receiving stations was more or less ten cents a pound. Vidal and Stella received $2.50 per pound after the coffee was roasted and packaged. Erick negotiated an agreement with the parish team that it would pay the same rate to small coffee growers that Vidal and Stella received; and Vidal and Stella agreed to process their coffee and sell it at country locations, so coffee not certified as organic would become part of the Don Justo inventory. When I retired in 2006, that agreement continued as part of the contractual agreement between all the parties involved. At some point, exactly when or why I am not sure, perhaps costs to the partner organizations, it was decided to terminate the part of Don Justo Coffee project that gave focus to the economic justice of the small coffee farmer.

Erick and Meredith were people of action, not words, and the team very much liked that about them. However, the disagreement that later would play into the contentious impasse that grew between them surfaced in a meeting just prior to their leaving to go home. Erick and Meredith had been adamant (with me) that the Compañeros would receive no money from the profits, even though the Compañeros had provided the opportunity for them to organize the business. Also many Presbyterian churches were involved with purchase of the coffee and Sue had designed the logo. In the meeting, it was the parish team that said the Compañeros would be included in the division of profits at the rate of fifty cents per pound. Erick and Meredith respected the parish team's request and complied without protest.

Erick enrolled in graduate school for his doctoral studies, and Meredith continued to be coordinator of sales, making several trips to Iowa from Ohio. It had been agreed by all parties that the parish team was the owner of record of the Don Justo Coffee business. To comply with that decision, Compañeros purchased the copyright for the logo in the parish team's name.

Within six months the parish team felt forced into a decision they would rather not have had to make. They received a copy of an email Meredith had written that had negative connotations about the Compañeros. The team asked me to excuse myself from the meeting. They did not want me to be party to the decision they felt necessary for the ongoing good of the project. After a lengthy discussion they, by consensus, wrote Erick and Meredith a letter asking them to no longer be involved with the project. The response by Erick and Meredith was to send an email to all churches that purchased coffee that announced an end to the project that they had built.

The Compañeros responded by sending a message to all churches they knew bought coffee to say it would continue as a parish team project with sales coordinated by the Compañeros. Some confusion about what was going on resulted in diminished sales. Meredith's charisma also played into a few churches' decisions to not buy Don Justo Coffee, because it just was not fair that she would be so summarily dismissed.

Don Justo Coffee continues to be sold in several Des Moines area churches, as well as in a couple of small businesses that do not require a bar code for inventory and sales records. In time, the parish team discontinued the purchase of Don Justo Coffee for a fair price from the small farmer, thus removing an essential source of income. Even though they still purchase and sell the coffee, through a larger farm, it contributes a negative image that makes me sad. But, even in the light of that negative, the profits to the parish team have provided much needed income for mission projects as well as to pay off the mortgage on the Casa Pastoral. And it continues today as a predictable income for project expenses in the cantónes.

Blanchard Court Bags A.K.A.. Blanca's Bags

Women who produce Blanca's Bags displaying handiwork

Blanca is the name that guarantees quality. If it has her name on it, she will have it no other way. A few months before I retired from working with the parish team in Berlin, they began a business known as Blanca's Bags. They are made from Salvadoran and Guatemalan fabric of multi-colored design. There are big bags, small bags, shoulder bags, handbags, coin bags, zipper bags, two-zipper bags; every style bag imaginable. In 2006, when I retired, all the bags were all handmade with quality workmanship by members of the parish team, as well as other women in the pueblo of Berlin, who were trained to sew them. Sadly, that is no longer true, as Blanca's Bags are now made in Guatemala, and purchased by the parish team as its inventory.

Blanca's Bags are famous among delegations that visit the Casa Pastoral. Anyone who asks will be given the opportunity to purchase bags from among the hundreds available. There was a time they would have HAD

TO have bought them to sell, as no one could sew with the confidence and precision necessary of the level of professional seamstresses, as shown by the quality of the bags. Lisa Bock of Chicago, IL., is the person who taught them to sew the beautiful bags they advertised and sold.

Lisa wanted to create a line of beautiful women's bags, quality bags sewn from imported hand- painted fabric. She designed a few, sewed a few and received accolades of praise for her work. But there was not enough time in the day that she herself could sew enough bags to make the endeavor worthwhile. Besides she had two young sons to care for. No matter how much passion she had for sewing beautiful bags, she had more passion to be the best mother in the world. Then she heard through her husband Mike of a way to realize her dream because of something he had been told by a fellow worker named Bill Fisher. Mike and Bill were both Xerox executives confined together in a car on their way to a company event. Mike told Bill about Lisa's dream to build a business of high-end women's bags. Bill told Mike about his dream to help the people of Berlin create a more just life. It was like the proverbial match made in heaven. If she was willing to go to El Salvador to teach women in the Berlin Community how to make the bags, she would have quality workmanship by women of conscience, and a product to sell. At the same time the women who did the work would receive more than a fair wage for their talent. It sounded like a viable option to Lisa, so plans were made for her to make a trip to Berlin, El Salvador, to teach selected women how to sew her design bags. Among those women was Blanca.

Lisa is a tall, pretty woman with an engaging smile. If there was any anxiety among the women of Berlin about what the relationship with Lisa would be like, it was quickly dispersed by her kind demeanor and her ability to communicate with them in Spanish. The day after she arrived at the Casa Pastoral, she set up sewing class in the garage and learning to sew her bags began. I could not begin to know all the dynamics of that teaching/learning experience, but I do know friendships began to form between the women of Berlin and Lisa, a gringa from Chicago, Illinois who believed in the ability of women of poverty to become professional seamstresses and produce a quality product. Not all the women who began the class felt the call to be professional in the work, so some of them dropped out early on. But those who persisted became more and more proficient at doing it Lisa's way, the quality way and the professional way. By the time Lisa left for home a few days later, Blanca had become "supervisor" of the women who would sew Blanchard Court Bags.

Lisa and Mike and their two sons lived in a house on Blanchard Court, in Wheaton, Illinois, thus the name, Blanchard Court Bags. Lisa made a trip to explain the project to several churches in the Des Moines area. Her commitment to build the business was expressed by her return to Berlin several times to do continuing education and to keep up morale of the women. She made sure they had the best equipment. She paid them exceedingly well for their labor. In return she expected, and received, quality work under the watchful eye of Blanca.

Christmas season came and Lisa had an open house in her home for Blanchard Court Bags. She laid out her product throughout the house decorated with a holiday theme. Many people came, business was brisk, and when the day was over she was happy about the sales she had made. It gave her and everyone involved reason to hope, although it was a cautious hope for Lisa, because it would take more bags than what they had produced that year to make it a business worth her time. Also there were the import requirements and the tax issues to resolve to be able to import large numbers of bags into the United States from El Salvador. But she entered another year with an expectant eye on the goal she had set for a high-end bag business that would give a good income to her and to the workers she had come to love so much.

Lisa continued the struggle a second year. The tax issue was a continuous issue. The quality of work was not a problem, but import of sufficient numbers of bags was a growing concern. A second Christmas came and the second open house held to promote the bags. I was there for that day and remember the high hopes for success as bags were arranged for sale in creative displays. At the end of the day, however, the results were not what Lisa had hoped for. I don't have a clear understanding of all the grounds for Lisa's allowing her vision of hope to become the impossible dream. Not long after that open house, Lisa told the parish team she would not continue the business. Blanca does not show much emotion. Her philosophy is life is what it is. Accept it. But that day she received the news about Lisa's decision to quit making bags, I saw a tear of sadness form as she looked into the northern sky toward the city of Chicago, where her friend Lisa lived, her friend whom she would likely never see again.

According to Einstein, matter cannot be destroyed, but only changed in form. Likewise, according to Blanca, Lisa's dream to create a beautiful line of bags cannot be destroyed, but only changed in design. I am not sure where the idea of Blanca's bags originated, but it was not difficult to convince Blanca that a line of bags in her name could be sold at the Casa Pastoral. I have learned to never assume that I know what motivates a person to make decisions in life, but Blanca's decision to allow the creation of Blanca's Bags, I cannot help but feel, is in part a memorial to Lisa, her dream, and her love for the people she taught to sew so well.

Chapter 15

My Family Grows (Unofficially)

No matter how you cut it, anyone born in the USA and even those who live under U.S. Government poverty guidelines are considered to be rich by 90 percent of the world's population. As a wealthy American, if you find yourself standing in the presence of Third World poverty so as to smell its stench and see the bloat of hunger and pleading eyes of those who suffer and not share your wealth, then your faith is as useless as yesterday's dishwater. When I lived El Salvador, I had to ask myself if saving for my retirement in the future was more urgent, more important than living my faith in the present. Poverty stood before me, represented by people I had come to know by name. Would I spend money I saved for future comfort and security to send poverty packing that hope might come into their lives? Would I conform to the ways of the world or be transformed by the renewal of my mind and follow the way of the cross?

At some point, I had to give up thinking about all the theories of life and death and respond to what was before me. The decision to cast my bread upon the waters and share what I had saved for retirement was a confirmation of my faith, but also it was a response to what my father, a poor man with meager resources, said to me nearly six decades before after I saw him give away his only good winter coat to a stranger: "Sometimes other people need what you have more than you do. I would like for you to never forget that."

The following stories are about five families in El Salvador who have become like my own children and grandchildren. I consider each of them to be gifts God set before me that I might know God's grace and forgiveness in the living of my faith, and rejecting arrogance of self-interest to be set free from the ways of the world.

Maria Isabel Tobar Amaya
A Heart of Faith, Courage and Love

A young woman's story of struggle and determination to honor her mother

Maria Isabel and Krystal

It is common to hear that behind every successful man is a capable, kind, and savvy woman. And so God created Eve. But the truth is that those women often stand alone, the sole defense of vulnerable loved ones. I have seen this truth over and over in my life, but perhaps the woman who most clearly demonstrates this for me is Maria Isabel Tobar Amaya. Her story speaks of the love and care mothers of the world should receive. It is also a story that demonstrates the personal hell that violence of war and civil unrest causes.

Maria Isabel is 25 years old but looks as if she is twenty, and weighs no more than 100 pounds soaking wet. She is a resident of Apopa, which is a gang-infested suburb of San Salvador. She speaks of God's love and faith in Jesus' promises to carry her through the tough times of life. This is her story.

When she was just a baby, one of her brothers was killed by the military during the civil war. He was one of the more than 75,000 civilian victims the violence of war claimed. Maria Isabel's mother went crazy with grief. But in time, she recovered, and Maria Isabel grew up in a loving family environment. Her mother took care of her and two sisters and one remaining brother. Her father held a responsible job, and the pain of the death the family experienced became a distant but sad memory. But that all fell apart beginning in 1999. Maria Isabel's one surviving brother was killed by one of the gangs, a social consequence of poverty and war that has become what I term as Central America's Street Mafia. The death of her second son pushed Maria Isabel's mother over the edge and mental illness took control of her life.

Her mother talks to herself incessantly. Sometimes she does not sleep, and cries far into the night. She has uncontrollable fits of violence and hits Maria Isabel when she is unable to comprehend what is happening. One day she was enraged by the sound of Maria Isabel's cell phone so threw it into a bucket full of water.

When Maria Isabel's mother became ill, her father demanded she get over it and become her old self. Like many people caught in the web of violence and the mental illness of loved ones, he could not face nor cope with the truth of his family's own tragedy. He began to drink heavily and frequently his own mental faculties were obliterated in a fog of inebriation. He lost his job. He quit providing financial support for Maria and her mother. To support his accelerating alcoholism, he sold the house from beneath them all, and he fled the household and found himself another woman. Maria Isabel's two sisters are married with children. She is the only one left at home. The burden of caring for her mother is hers alone to bear. She took her mother to a doctor to see if she could be committed for medical care. She was told no, because they had on money to pay for her care.

It was at that stage of her life that I came to know Maria Isabel. I had gone to the chapel at the Divina Providencia, where Monsignor Oscar Romero had been martyred. There she was on her knees praying for strength and courage. One of the nuns at the chapel explained briefly Maria Isabel's circumstances and asked if there was some way I could help. So began my friendship with Maria Isabel. For $300 we were able to get Maria and her mother into a safe and comfortable, although small home. The mortgage on the home is $50 per month.

With a home, life for them stabilized somewhat. I send $100 to Maria Isabel each month so she has money for rent and some food. She is an educated hairdresser and is able to find work now and then to pay other bills. When I am in El Salvador, I make sure I have lunch with Maria Isabel. I consider her one of my Salvadoran daughters. When I visit their home, I take apples to her mother. It is one of her favorite fruits. She always tells me to take the apples and get out of their home. Once in a while, though, after a visit with Maria Isabel, when I get ready to leave she shakes my hand and gives me a feeble smile. Always she holds tight onto the apples. Maria Isabel exemplifies how necessary are courage, faith, and love in very trying times. With courage, she has taken responsibility for her mother (she calls her mommy), with occasional support from the rest of her family and has kept her from falling off the edge. And she is unwilling to walk away from what many would consider an impossible dream, that is, to make her mother well. Such faith as this gives hope in the face of despair. It is my prayer that the love Maria Isabel so freely gives in the care of her mother will ultimately provide the joy and peace she so desperately wants for her mother and herself. I help to ensure she has a home where she can care for not only her mother, but also her daughter, and. Krystal, to whom Maria Isabel gave birth October 1, 2008. Maria Isabel calls me Papa, Krystal's grandpa.

Erick Hernesto Martinez Mindez
studying to be a psychologist
A story about a lad who went from the streets to the university

Erick, Esmerelda and Cesar

Erick was not exactly on the streets when I met him. He lived with his grandmother up the mountain from Berlin, on the way to the cross that had been placed above the pueblo by the Parish of Saint Joseph. It was a favorite hiking destination for many. He lived with his grandmother in one of the huts by the tower that you would pass by on your way to the cross.

I saw Erick often in the park soliciting shoe shine business that helped to pay the bare necessities for him and his grandmother. He was a stocky boy, thirteen years old with a shy smile and a hint of sadness that looked out at you under the brim of his always-present baseball cap. His wide forehead and square chin suggested he one day could be a boxer if he became more assertive and threatening. But the silent sadness defined a reserved personality that made him inconspicuous in a crowd. Erick's life was a prime case for gang recruitment, especially so when his grandmother died. Erick's personality had been defined by a series of life experiences that no little boy should ever have to endure. His father had been killed in the war when he was a toddler. Not long after that his mother ran off to who knows where, leaving him in the care of his frail, elderly grandmother. Every day she would make her way down to the pueblo where she sold fruit and vegetables in the market. Erick shined shoes in the park to make what he could for household expenses. Between the two of them they staved off hunger barely.

Near the end of October, 2003, a visitor came knocking at the door of the Casa Pastoral. It was Erick, and he asked to speak with me. He was polite and direct. "Can I borrow $10?" he asked, and immediately launched into an explanation why he was asking. The next day was Day of the Dead, when everyone in El Salvador goes to the cemetery to celebrate the lives of their loved ones who have died. They trim the grass on the grave, plant flowers, paint the tombstone, make needed repairs, and even have a meal at the grave. Erick wanted the money to buy a gallon of paint and a brush so he could hire out as a tombstone painter. He assured me he would pay me back the very next day as soon as he was through with all the work he was certain he would have from painting tombstones. It struck me as quite an enterprising endeavor, and I agreed to the loan. His parting words were, "I will see you tomorrow. Thanks for the loan." The next day Erick was a no-show.

It was not the money, but the principle that Erick not only failed to pay the loan, but also that he turned and went the other way when I saw him in the market. He successfully avoided me for several weeks until one day I rounded a corner and ran smack-dab into him. With no place to run, he profusely apologized for failing to pay me the loan I had made to him. Clearly the reason was that the work painting tombstones did not materialize. He told me he still had the paint. He would be glad to bring it to me. But he had no idea where he would get the money to pay me $10. He was remorseful and polite and I had no intention of making life difficult for him. We agreed on a plan that would allow him to pay the debt. He would come to the Casa Pastoral every Tuesday at five p.m. and shine my shoes. Each shine would reduce the debt he owed by fifty cents, the cost of a shoe shine in the park.

Erick showed up on time the following Tuesday. I gave him my shoes and said he could leave them on the steps when he finished. A half hour later I found the shoes cleaned and shined with a hand written note that read, "Thank you, Hermano Roberto," a courtesy I could not ignore. I asked Blanca to tell me what she knew about the lad. Then I knew Berlin was not unlike small town Iowa, where everyone knows your name and tragedies that have brought struggle and sadness into your life. She told me Erick's childhood story. Erick's knock on the door of the Casa Pastoral several weeks ago now came knocking at the door to my heart. It was easy for that door to open to him. That night I made a promise that whenever possible, I would sit with Erick while he shined my shoes.

The following Tuesday I sat with Erick while he worked at putting a shiny luster on my shoes. I sensed he was a little unsure why I was there and our conversation was limited his answers to my questions: How are you doing? Is business in the park good? Where do you live? The next week Erick had prepared his mind and soul for conversation with the gringo. When I sat down next to him, he was the one to begin asking the questions about my life, my country and why was I in Berlin.

For several weeks we got to know each other in conversation while he shined my shoes. About the ninth week, I relinquished my demand for full repayment of the loan and suggested he continue to come each Tuesday and I would pay him in cash. The debt had been paid. He grinned, shook my hand and asked, "Can I call you Papa? I don't have a papa of my own." I said "Yes, Erick, and I will tell people that you are my son from El Salvador." To this day we have that understanding for our relationship.

I asked Erick about school. He said he wanted to continue studying in high school next year when he was through with junior high, but he could not afford it. I told him I would pay his cost. He smiled broad. Silence grew loud between us, but it was a good silence, a contented silence, like that in which you hear God's still small voice. That night when Erick finished he said, "Thank you, Papa." Then he hugged me.

Erick did well in high school. He kept me posted by faithfully bringing me his report card at the end of each quarter. He wanted to join the band and play the base drum. I paid the cost for him to join the band. He needed tennis shoes for P.E. class. I paid the cost of his tennis shoes. Time flew by and before we knew it, Erick was facing graduation from high school at the end of the year. Though it was February and there were several months until graduation, I could tell there was something on his mind. I encouraged him with one of those parental, "What is it Erick? What is on your mind?" College was what was on his mind. Instinctively, he knew that was more money than I could afford, but Erick had taken up residence in my heart and I was not about to say no to his dream. So I did the other parental thing, "We will see, Erick."

I pondered and prayed, but from human analysis Erick's college dream was hopeless. In March of the year, Erick graduated from high school. The annual delegation from the University of Iowa Wesley Foundation, led by United Methodist pastor and campus minister Marsha Acord, made their annual visit to Berlin. One or two of the students spoke Spanish and Erick came to shine my shoes like he always did on Tuesday evenings. Naturally, they began to converse and that exchange grew into a friendship between them. That night they wanted to know more about Erick, so I told them his story and ended with his dream to attend the university. The students wanted to pay his way, and Marsha's kind heart was captured between wanting to say yes and wondering how that would be paid for. But, they left with a tentative agreement that the U of I students, through the Wesley Foundation, would pay Erick's university costs. It is a faith commitment that has been kept for four years with intentions of paying Erick's next two years toward a degree to become a psychologist. The kind generosity of Marsha and all the students will give him a well deserved title of Dr. Erick Mindez.

Erick's first year of studying at the university in San Miguel was a lonely one, and he came to me and said he had friends in Oregon who had invited him to come live with them. Would I buy him some good boots for the journey? I told him no. As his papa, I did not agree to such a decision as that. Plus, why would he give up a coveted university education just to go be with friends in a country where he would not be welcome without a visa? He never broached the topic again, and within a few months Erick had met the love of his life, Esmerelda, a beautiful indigenous woman who has given birth to their son, Cesar. Erick still calls me papa and grandpa to his son. Esmerelda has the same shy demeanor, as did Erick when I met him. She, too, had a life of sadness caused by her father being killed and her mother running off, leaving her in the hands of her grandmother. They are a team, Esmerelda and Erick. They make me proud to call them my Salvadoran family, soon to be known as Dr. Erick and Esmerelda Mindez and son Cesar.

Erica Christina Bonilla Garcia
Widowed by gang members Who had no pity
Thirteen Bullets that Turned Hopeful Struggle to Tragic Despair

Erica, Umberto and children

Of all those I call my children in El Salvador, I have known Erica the longest. I met her as she was selling newspapers at the stoplight of Avenida Bernal and San Antonio Abad. She is a pretty woman with long black hair that she pulls into a pony tail. She has a genuine smile that accentuates a kind personality. She has three children; a girl twelve and two boys seven and four. Her husband Umberto was shot thirteen times by two gang members in 2008 while he was selling newspapers at the same stoplight as Erica. He had denounced the "brotherhood" a few months prior, said he did not want to belong to the gang anymore. Such a decision is akin to treason. Traitors are shot. So on a Sunday morning in 2008, with his entire family watching a car pulled up, and he was shot thirteen times in the head and chest. Erica's fear, caused by her husband's murder, drove her to abandon the home she had grown to love so much and flee with her children to Soyapango to live with her mother in a tiny two bedroom cinder block home.

In early December, 2001, I was in San Salvador. The corner where Erica sold newspapers was half a block from where I slept when I went to San Salvador, so that is where I always went for my morning newspaper to go with my cup of coffee. It was always a moment of brevity as Erica would taunt me about my accent but her kind smile told me she thought I was a nice man. That morning in early December, when I saw Erica she did not have to tell me there was something wrong. She did not smile nor look me in the eye when she handed me the newspaper. With my question if she had a problem came a flood of tears. Between sobs she told how she and the family were going to be put out of the home where they lived. The owner had come by the night before and told them they had to move so he could put the house up for sale. If they had to move, they had no money to pay a deposit, which was always required, and she was afraid they would wind up in the street. I asked her how much it would cost if they had the money. The cost was $500.00. It hardly seemed possible that one could buy a home at such a low price but when I saw it, I understood. It was a one-room cinder block home with an unfinished dirt floor enclosed area behind it where there was a bathroom. I guess the adage, "home is where your heart is" applied, as they were happy beyond words when I gave them the money to make the purchase. Neither Erica nor Umberto knew their fathers, and so they began to call me papa.

Each time I was in San Salvador I would buy fruit and vegetables at a stand near their home and take them to Erica. One time when I visited, I found Umberto's mother had become part of the household, and not long after that Erica was pregnant with their third child. From the perspective of a gringo, they needed more room to be comfortable. I suggested if they would finish the dirt floor room attached to the house that they would more than double their living space. I could tell such a project was beyond their knowing where to begin, so that afternoon I sent a man who knew construction to their home to make an estimate on cost of remodeling. The price came back at $1500.00. A couple weeks later I went to see them and asked how they felt about borrowing the $1500.00 from me at 4% interest. The interest thing bothered Erica, as though there had been a time when interest on a loan had become a big problem. But I assured her it would not be like that this time, and the trust level between us made the deal possible. We wrote up a contract for the loan and a contractor was hired to do the work. Two months later, the living space for them was doubled and Erica said she felt like she lived in a castle compared to what it had been before with one room.

The new room was finished by the time the Drake University delegation visited El Salvador under the sponsorship of St. Catherine Parish and the leadership of Fr. Jim Larenzo. Always the delegation wanted a work day as part of their itinerary. I told Jim about Erica and Umberto and the house they had remodeled. It needed painting. And what would really be nice is if a gas stove and a refrigerator could be included in the budget, as they had only a hotplate to cook on and no refrigerator at all. Fr. Jim said yes. Fr. Jim has a big heart for the poor and is an easy touch.

The delegation of ten students, and 3 faculty supervisors, worked all day on the job. The new paint over the dreary gray of cinder block had brightened the house considerably. Umberto was so overcome with gratitude with the project that he felt compelled to express it with a hug for everyone who was there. But the best was yet to come, with delivery of a stove and refrigerator. Erica and Umberto had not been told about the gifts. I called for the delivery that was waiting nearby and soon two men with a stove and a refrigerator on two-wheelers came down the sidewalk. Erica stepped into the doorway to allow room for them to pass by. Her expression of disbelief, her hand held over her mouth in surprise was a statement beyond words of her gratitude when I told her she was in the way of the delivery into her house. In that moment, according to Erica and Umberto, they had received gifts beyond the value of everything they had ever owned.

I will always wonder how much this improvement in standard of living played into Umberto's decision to renounce his gang membership. He did not say that is why and I have never felt comfortable asking Erica if it did. For whatever reason he knew he was violating the rules of gang membership, but still he was compelled to do it. I was in El Salvador visiting at the time of his death. Erica called me with the news and I could hear along with the grief that overwhelmed her something else. It was fear. How would she ever be able to provide for the children by herself?

And so I told her that is what grandpas are for, to make sure their grandchildren have food for the table. I asked her to promise to do all she could to find work to provide income but that she could depend on me for a monthly income to help her with expenses. Of the five families in El Salvador who have become like my children and grandchildren, I worry most about Erica and her children. For them I see no way out of the poverty that traps them. At night when I consider the lives of all those people who have touched mine, it is Erica and her children who remind me life is not fair and sometimes it is so cruel so as to bring silent sobs in the night. Erica fled with her children to find what comfort a mother can give her children and grandchildren. When I visit them on trips to El Salvador I see the stove and refrigerator Erica brought with her that she says are her proof that miracles can happen.

Flor Daniela Lemus Navas
A woman who never knew her father, was orphaned at the age of 3, and raised her two older sisters on the streets of San Salvador

The story of a woman who lives with the belief "siempre hay soluciones" always there are solutions

Daniela, Dayana, Daniel and Carlos Daniela's Children

I found the name of the cemetery, "Jardínes de Recuerdo" in the yellow pages. It is at the entrance to San Salvador on the road from the airport. I called the number and asked to speak with someone about costs. I had been considering options for disposing of my body should I die in El Salvador, including the cost of sending the body back to the U.S. or having it cremated and part of the ashes sent, with some of them to be buried in the chapel floor at Our Sister Parish Mission. I waited several minutes on the line and was about to hang up to try another day when I heard a woman's voice. "Hola. Soy Daniela. Mucho gusto." The person who had answered the phone had explained to her my situation and she said we should meet to discuss the various options and costs. Ultimately, after meeting with her, I purchased a burial plan for cremation, with part of the ashes going to Berlin and part coming back to the U.S. for burial in the Dexter cemetery. I no longer have that plan, but I retain the relationship that developed when I went searching for answers to questions I had about death in El Salvador.

When The Sun Comes Up in the West

Daniela was persistent in making sure I had all the information I needed to make a decision. She was not pushy but was not about to let this sale get away, and after four conversations with her, I was comfortable with my decision to buy a plan I could buy on time using an automatic withdrawal on my credit card. I could drop it any time I wished, but it guaranteed a plan for burial without a huge initial investment. We set the meeting to sign the contract at the cemetery office, but the morning of the signing, she called to see if either we could set another time, or if I was OK with it, for me to come to her home to sign the contract as she had no one to take care of little Daniel, who was two years old. Since I was in San Salvador and I wanted to get the deal done, I agreed to meet her at her home. In that meeting, at her home, I met the real Daniela. She was a peasant woman struggling to care for her two children, Daniel, age two, and Dayana, age eight. She brought me a cup of coffee and apologized she did not have any milk for the coffee but had a bit of sugar if I wanted it sweet. A cantaro and gallon jugs suggested she carried water, and when I asked, she admitted she carried it from a neighbor, since hers had been shut off for non-payment of the bill. Her rather elegant dress at the cemetery belied the truth of her real life.

Her husband had been killed at a car wash a few months after Daniel's birth. Dayana's father wasn't even around for the birth and had since told her not to bother him about the child that he wanted nothing to do with either of them. An intruder had shot her mother in the head when she was three years old, and she never knew her father. She had two older sisters she had lived with when young, but mainly she took care of herself growing up. I asked her what her dream would be if she could have anything she wanted. Her answer was a visa to the United States. I told her I had no authority over issuance of visas, but how about I paid the water bill instead? I gave her $100 and told her to buy some milk for the children with the $40-plus dollars left over. I could see signs of malnourishment and knew they needed more than milk.

By the time I had contacted Daniela about burial plans, I had made the decision to share my wealth where it seemed important to do so. I have found that importance in her situation. Like I did with Erica and Umberto, I felt compelled to take fruit and vegetables to Daniela, too. I watched the apparent malnutrition signs disappear and her children looked healthier and had more energy than when I met them. They began to be more and more comfortable with me, and then one time as I was leaving after dropping off some groceries, Dayana said she wanted to talk with me. We went to the patio and she asked if I would be her Padrino, which is godfather, when she joined the church. I said yes, and she said, "Gracias, abuelo." Thank you, Grandfather.

Daniela is a pretty woman who always struggled to keep from gaining weight. She never had any problem finding a boyfriend. But she never kept them long. One in particular I liked very much. He was respectful and good to the children. He truly seemed to love them all and I thought it was her opportunity for marriage. But one day, like the two or three others I had known over a year or two, he was gone. I had stopped by with some groceries and we talked about her relationships that kept disappearing. I asked her why, and especially with the last one. She said, "I want to marry you."

I had to sit down. After the shock of what I heard had settled I told her I did not think that was a good idea. I had not been thinking about marriage, and actually had no desire to do it again, after being divorced twice. I was much older than she and I likely would not live in El Salvador the rest of my life. To which she said she would promise to take good care of me, that the children really loved me, she did not care about the age difference, and if she was married to me, she would get a visa as my wife. Then she would have her dream, which was to live in the United States. Bingo! Daniela's solution for getting a visa was to marry me.

It was stupid of me not to say no right then and there. But Daniela is a persuasive woman, and my ego got in the way of logic. I told her I would think about it and even went so far as to announce to some in the U.S. that I would be getting married. The parish team was as persuasive in helping me see the reality of what I was thinking as Daniela was in talking me into it. And besides, as godfather to Dayana, the church forbade me to enter into marriage with the mother of the child. It did not take much for them to convince me that was not a very good idea and, in the end, I dodged that bullet.

Daniela was always looking for the solution that would stabilize her life. Finally she hit on one. She learned the car import business. She purchased wrecked cars in the U.S., had them shipped to El Salvador, had them repaired at a body shop and sold them, using some of the proceeds to repeat the process. Being in the car business, it was a natural she would meet a man who was an announcer on a radio program that announced car racing. His name is Carlos and she bore a child by him whose name is Carlito or Carlos Jr.

When I became Dayana's godfather, I told Daniela I would pay for the cost of education for her and Daniela in a private school. Each month I send her $300 for that purpose. I believe education is the way out of poverty, and if they have the best education, they have a better chance of rising above where they have been to be successful in making a better life for their future. Daniela continues to search for the solution that will stabilize her life economically. Today she owns a small used clothing store on Boulevard Constitution, just a few blocks from where Umberto (from the previous story about Erica) was gunned down by gangs. She is still quite young, and it is my hope she will find her niche in the business world that will give her the ultimate in success that she feels will be the final solution to lift her out of the poverty she has known all her life. And by the way, she did, four years ago, succeed in getting a ten-year visa to the United States. That was a sign for me that Daniela will, in the end, be the winner in the game of life.

Roxana Lucia Marmol
A woman 33 years old, who looks 23, raising four teenagers by herself

The story of a young woman's struggle to keep her four teenage children from a life in the streets

Roxana with her four children

The one-cup coffee maker had just stopped perking when I heard a knock on the door. I did not know anyone personally in the gated community in Soyapango, where I had rented an apartment for when came to San Salvador. So I was a little nervous when the knock came and was grateful for the peep-hole in the door to see who was there. I could see the face of a young woman, pretty, looking at the peep-hole as though she could see through it to the inside. I left the door chained but cracked it so I could speak with her. Maybe she is a woman, but that did not mean she had good intentions. She responded to my greeting by telling me her name was Roxana and that Daniela, our mutual friend, had given her my name and that she should come see me. Thanks, Daniela, I thought. I briefly thought about asking her to come back later after I had finished my coffee. I am always in a better mood after I have had coffee in the morning. But, instead, I unhooked the chain to let her into a living room littered with yesterday's newspaper and laundry to be done.

Roxana is pretty, easy to talk with, flirts well, and right away I could see I was in trouble. From the first word out of her mouth, she had my attention. Daniela was one of her good friends, and she explained, "When we were talking last night about stuff, your name came up and she mentioned you live here and it is close to my home and that I should come talk to you." I still didn't know what she was getting at but I knew that "stuff" could mean problems and "I should talk to you" means the problem has to do with money, so likely she came to me because she wants me to help her with a problem that requires money.

I want to take a moment for a tangential comment here for anyone reading this: Remember, tip of the iceberg means exactly that--you are seeing (hearing) only about 10 percent of the problem/issue/situation/whatever it is the person came to speak with you about. And, oh yes, photos. If they bring photos to talk about the problem/issue/situation, it means the children are adorable and will most certainly eat their way into your heart. And you always should know the problem/issue/situation is serious and not something you can easily dismiss and not think about when someone knocks on a perfect stranger's door at 8 a.m. to tell him about it.

Roxana lined the photos up on the coffee table, oldest to youngest. And then she cried. In a nutshell, her husband had left her more than a year ago to live in Mexico. He sends her no financial support. She could not pay all the fees to the school by the end of school year last year and now they can't attend school because of what she owes, and they are going to be on the street. (the reader should know "on the street" for pretty young girls is another way of saying they will soon be in gangs or prostitution.) My heart ached for Roxana. And the first words out of my mouth were, "We will figure something out." And her response was, "Daniela told me you would say that."

Well, as a matter of fact, or an act of grace, we did figure it out. Roxana owed the school $600 to catch up from last year and to pay the cost of entering school for the year. I asked and received permission from the school principal to pay the amount in two payments. The children were in school. Over the next year I learned more about Roxana's plight.

She lost the home they had lived in for thirteen years to the bank for not being able to pay the mortgage. She moved to a rental house and during a major storm it flooded, ruining all the personal possessions she had accumulated over those thirteen years. She moved from that house, which had essentially been destroyed, to a patio behind an internet café which gave her two small bedrooms, a bathroom, and small kitchen. And she had no consistent income, although she tried selling organic products on the street.

I asked her, as I ask everyone I seek to help, "What is your dream?" She said she wanted to go to school to be a beautician. It cost $280 for nine months. I told her I would pay the cost of her school. But, she said, likely she was going to jail for non-payment of a loan she took out three years ago to try to make money repairing cars and selling them. It worked well for a while she said, and then the economy collapsed. I asked her how much the loan payment was. It was $300 per month. I send Roxana $750 per month to pay for her children's education, the cost of her beauty school, and the loan to the bank. I cannot do it forever, and she knows that. She hopes to up a beauty salon in a room in the front of the home where they lives in order to make a living. The cost of the salon is $3,300. I asked her why she does not just go get a job at an existing beauty salon. She clearly states to me the two reasons why this is not good: (1) Working for someone else pays far less than she is sure she can make in her own business. But, more importantly, (2) she wants to be close to home to keep an eye on (translated protect) her young teenage daughters who are vulnerable to macho behavior of men in El Salvador. I get it. Her children call me Grandpa. She calls me Papa. Do you think I am going to allow that to happen to my granddaughters? You can bet your life I am not. What kind of a Papa would I be to allow something like that? I remain committed to paying the cost of her children's education. God willing, Roxana's business will begin earning what she needs to be comfortable in life and pay off the bank loan on her own.

Es la vida.

A Fund has been established for continued support of the families in El Salvador mentioned above, for when I am no longer able to provide for them. Successor Advisors have been named to carry on the intent of the fund.

The Robert C. Cook Fund for Salvadoran Family Dignity is administered by The Community Foundation of Greater Des Moines, 1915 Grand Avenue, Des Moines, IA 50309. Donations are tax deductable and are very much appreciated. Donations should be made to the Greater Des Moines Foundation, noted to be for the fund in my name. Profits from this book will also be donated to that foundation.

Chapter 15

Postscript
Undocumented Immigrants

Economics of Government Policies and Private Investments:
Forum on Latin America Issues May, 2008
At Highland Park Presbyterian Church, Des Moines, Iowa

My name is Robert Cook. I am the stated supply pastor here at Highland Park Presbyterian Church. Welcome to this forum on Latin America issues. Rev. Gil Dawes will talk Panama, Richard Flamer will talk about the Chiapas area of Mexico and the Guatemala–Mexican border, and. I will be talking about El Salvador.

Tonight's forum was put together by some folks who are concerned about the way immigrants are being treated in Iowa and around the nation and felt it important for the reality from which they come in Latin America be discussed and why they would make such an expensive and dangerous trek in the first place. It is essential information in the age-old question about survival of the hungry and poor. The format for this evening will be a ten to fifteen minute presentation about each of the countries I mentioned. Then you will have time to dialogue about the political and economic conditions raised and the impact they have on the Latin American populations, both there and here.

I returned from a brief visit to El Salvador this month (May, 2008). Many of you here have visited that country and know the population of nearly 6.5 million people fits into a very small space of 12,400 square miles, a space about one-sixth the size of Iowa. To say the economy is weak is an understatement, and it is not an overstatement to say the fears of the poor, which are 60 percent of that country's population are very high, caused by the rapid increase in cost of living, especially in areas of food and transportation. The seven-member parish team in Berlin, where I served as Des Moines Presbytery's Designated Missionary for six years say that people are poorer and hungrier than they were at the beginning of the twelve-year-long civil war in 1980.

The median income of the urban dwellers is $157 per month. The median income in the country where agriculture is the main source of income is $80 per month. Half the population of 6.5 million people lives on less than $2 per day. Unemployment runs near 30 percent.

The week I came home, the newspaper headlines in one of the Salvadoran national newspapers, La Prensa, read that bus fares would increase by ten cents, from twenty-five to thirty-five cents. That is in the city. The increase will be more for those traveling longer distances to the country where many of the maquilas exist. Maquilas are essentially sweatshops that produce brand name clothing for export. The wage for those who sew that clothing is $150 per month. The cost of transportation to the maquilas will be as much as $24 more per month.

Food cost is the wolf that is looming outside the door of the poor. As with every trip I make to El Salvador, I visited the five families I support in El Salvador. I also had a conversation with Leslie Schuld, director of the Center for International Solidarity in El Salvador. There was agreement that food costs have increased by 50 percent in a short time. A newspaper article in La Prensa Graphica on May 16 attributes the increase to bad climate, demand for imports from Asian countries, and use of grains for biofuels. It detailed what it described as an extraordinary rise in food costs, which includes a 56 percent rise in corn (the basic grain for making tortillas) and 107 percent rise in beans, another basic food for the poor. A march for hunger in San Salvador, in which there were thousands participating, suggests the fear in the hearts of the poor in El Salvador, and there are predictions that the incidence of malnutrition will rise accordingly. The estimated twelve thousand children that die each year of malnutrition related causes would undoubtedly rise.

In the midst of this rapid cost of basic needs for the poor is the issue of immigration. It is estimated that seven hundred Salvadorans leave their homes daily to make their way north to the U.S. You are well aware of the government's recent raid in Postville near Waterloo, and the political outcry about the "illegal immigrants," as they call them, who are flooding into the country, supposedly causing great national security problems. Why are they attempting to emigrate here? Because over the past fifteen years the agriculture economy of that country was systematically dismantled by the wealthy so that the only option many have is to go where jobs are, which is here in the U.S. It was deliberate to create an import economy dependent on masses of people sending money from the U.S.

An explanation of how that was created is given in an article by Cesar Villalina entitled "Notes on the 'Agricultural Problem' – A History and Abstract of the Current Crisis in Agriculture in El Salvador." In it he states, "In 1990, the agricultural sector was taking in 20 percent of the bank credit and the country was producing 95 percent of the corn, rice, and beans that it was consuming. A total of 550,000 Salvadorans were living on food produced in the country and agriculture provided 17 percent of the gross national product."

With the signing of peace accords in 1992, the option was given for distribution of land to small farmers. The fourteen families that owned and controlled the land saw the writing on the wall and decided to diversify into other areas. One of them was importation of grains, fruits, and vegetables. So, the ruling ARENA political party made a series of "adjustments" that changed the agriculture productivity of the country. I take these statistics from Cesar Villalina's article.

- Interest rates went from 12 percent in 1989 to 21 percent in 2000, with the privatization of the national bank.
- There was a drop in loans to the small farmer due to the fact that the bank would not lend to the less profitable sectors

of the economy. Agriculture lost profitability and began to be replaced by imports made possible by massive imports that were allowed with the reduction of tariffs during the 1990s.

- The government reduced support to institutions related to agriculture, which in turn supported the small farmer. The percentage of the national budget dedicated to the Ministry of Agriculture and Livestock decreased from 4.2 percent in 1992 to 1.1 percent in 2007. The government almost completely dismantled the National Center for Agricultural and Forest Technology. In 1996 the Center helped small farmers through 78 extension offices and had a staff of 900, of whom 650 were technicians. Currently there are 31 extensions and 20 of those only provide two technicians.

According to Cesar Villalina's study what this caused is:

- Internal agriculture production fell from 17 percent of the Gross National Product in 1990 to 11 percent today.

- A reduction of 23 percent of land planted for goods for internal consumption that brought a drastic decrease in production of basic grains, basic crops, milk and meat.

- An increase in imported foods. Today 74 percent of the rice, 45 percent of the corn and 18% of beans that are consumed in El Salvador are imported as well as 60 percent of vegetables. Remember, I said earlier that in 1990, 95 percent of the country's basic grain, vegetable and fruit needs were met internally.

- Bankruptcy of small farmers that produced the corn, beans and rice forced them to move to the city to look for jobs. Jobs were not available. Today 3.5 million Salvadorans live in the city, many of them unemployed. To make it worse, education traditionally, especially in the country, went no higher than sixth grade, thus ensuring cheap labor for the wealthy. But it has created a limited educated population that is not conducive to industry establishing work opportunities.

The essential reality of the 1990s is that in this period, imports grew and production of basic foods decreased. The bankruptcy of the small farmer was deliberate so that the oligarchy, which for the last century lived on production of coffee and for which the price had fallen, made incursions into the business of basic grains without leaving the coffee business. The development of that business focused on import of basic grains, not production of them. Former president Christiani formed Arrocera San Francisco, an importer of grains, vegetables, and meats. The persons tied to the land were driven to bankruptcy. With unemployment high and minimum wage so little no one could survive, 2.5 million Salvadorans to date have made the decision to emigrate to the U.S. simply so their families can eat and have a roof over their heads. The money, called remittances by the system, maintains their lives, but they also maintain an import economy not a productive economy. So, folks, those who emigrate from El Salvador to the U.S. to work were forced to do so by a deliberate adjustment of production, because Christiani and others of his ilk can sell much more imported goods than they can produce. Thus, they make more money.

The crisis of hunger already exists. But the crisis will become much greater when the flow of dollars to the Salvadoran economy decreases and it becomes difficult to import basic goods. I know. Times are tough all over. And there is discontent about the rise in the cost of living here, too. But at least there is a cost of living increase in your salary and the impact of rising food and gasoline costs are more an irritation than a cause of fear in our hearts about survival. We already understand, by deliberate structural changes in the economy, the Salvadoran rich have created a need for men and women to emigrate to the U.S. to be able to survive. Go north, young man and woman. Get a job and send money home. Pay a coyote $6,000 to get to the U.S. Make that dangerous trip where you have a 95 percent chance of being raped if you are a woman, and who knows how many die of hunger and dehydration in the desert. The economy of El Salvador would teeter on collapse without the remittances. Fifteen percent of the gross domestic product of El Salvador is created by money sent back from the United States, according to Bishop Rosa Chavez, bishop of San Salvador.

The political and economic interest in remittances that essentially is El Salvador's economic survival is emphasized by newspaper reports about the rise and fall in the amounts sent. Again, an article in the La Presensa Graphica on May 16, 2008, had the headline "Remittances increase by 6.9 percent in April. It detailed not only that $313,000,000 was sent each month this year, but also talked about the rate of higher unemployment of Hispanics in the U.S., although it did not detail that percent of unemployment.

Finally, I want to mention briefly the political situation in El Salvador. It is an election year in El Salvador. There are two principle political parties, ARENA and FMLN. ARENA is what I would describe as the Republican Party and FMLN as the Democratic Party. The U.S. has made no secret that it is on the side of ARENA. In the Presidential election in 2004, the U.S. State Department sent Jeb Bush and a man whose last name is Noriega from the Department of Latino Affairs to deliver the message to the people. They said in public media that if FMLN candidate were elected, then family and friends in the U.S. would be denied the right to send money home to loved ones, and El Salvador would be treated as a terrorist country. This year the economy is causing the people to take a closer look at the candidates. The ARENA party has nominated former chief of the national police, Rodrigo Avila. He has become wealthy through ownership of the largest private security agency in El Salvador. He was part of death squad murders in the war, and he has intimidating capacity with the contacts he has with police, security and continuing death squads. His FMLN opposition is Maurico Funes. Maurico is a well-known, respected, and straight-talking reporter who pulls no punches. Many people say the murder of his son the week he announced his candidacy was no coincidence. ARENA is feeling the political pinch, and it warrants us keeping tabs on how things develop over the next year as they campaign in that country. What I heard from more than one person when I was there a couple weeks ago was "Maurico Funes will be the next president of El Salvador, if they don't kill him first."

Rev. Robert C. Cook

I approach this question of Salvadoran immigration from a biblical justice perspective. Immigrants are refugees seeking survival resources for themselves and their families. Old Testament as well as New is clear about welcoming the stranger that is among you. Immigrants are strangers that deserve that welcome. They are not terrorists, as suggested by some political rhetoric. They are refugees who have been forced into that situation by economic policies and political motives of both their homeland and by U.S. foreign trade policies. What happened to our tradition of welcoming the stranger into our midst, like we did the Southeast Asians after the Vietnam War? What happened to our ethics of caring for the weak and powerless and the poor? What happened to our policy of seeking justice for those who have been taken advantage of? When did the hearts of those who decide such policy turn to stone?

Acknowledgements

I know Doug Maben is a man of his word. So, when he offered to edit the story of the time that I lived in El Salvador, I knew it was not idle chat, but rather a promise. It was in August, 2006, when I had come to Iowa from El Salvador to prepare for retirement. Doug came out from Denver, Colorado, in order to attend the official ceremony of retirement from ministry that would take place at the meeting of the Presbytery of Des Moines. Duane, known by his close friends as "Doc," and Sheryll Skidmore, opened their home to for us for hospitality. It was there, with three of my best friends, that I began recounting to them, long into the night, my life and experiences as a missionary to El Salvador. It was that night that the Skidmores encouraged me to make my memories into a book.

The clincher came when Doug, in a moment of slight inebriation and tiredness from the day, offered a gift of incalculable worth of both time and energy, in saying he would be willing to edit what I wrote. In the time it has taken to create this offering, I suspect he has sworn many time over to keep his mouth shut when his foot is near. Thank you, Doc, Sheryll, and Doug. And, my acknowledgements could not be complete without mention of Jacque, the wonderful woman who is on a life's journey with Doug. To her I say thank you for giving up the considerable amount time that Doug could have spent with you, in order to make it a gift to me.

When I mentioned to friends about my plan to write a book, their question often, "What was I going to use to write it?' Many over the years have known me to be rather technologically challenged. However, that question that had been answered months before by Jeff Heil of Marshalltown, Iowa. He was a participant on the last delegation I led as missionary in El Salvador. I met Jeff's question of what I was planning to do in retirement, with mention of a dream I had of writing my memoirs. The day that he left to go home, at the airport, he handed me an envelope with a rather large sum of money; he told me to buy a good, functioning computer that would be capable of doing word processing. To Jeff, I say thank you, not only for your generous gift that made this work possible, but also for believing in my dream which, in turn, encouraged me to believe in it, too.

I wrote the book, and then learned that only about one percent of books written are published without a considerable investment of money. Predictably, when we tried to publish within our own lodge at Presbyterian Publishing House, we were flatly turned down; so much for having friends in high places. Doug informed me by phone of the rejection, in words unrepeatable here, and that he had discovered another potential publisher that we might try. They would help us self-publish and hopefully the book would be picked up by their parent publisher, Thomas Nelson. He suggested we put together a fund-raising gathering to "Get Bob's Book Out."

At the time he called, I was sitting at the kitchen table of Kathy and Jerry Burger. They live on a hog farm south of Waukee near I-80. Jerry had invited me to come and talk with them about the country of El Salvador that had become a cherished piece of their hearts since visiting the country. I want to say, in as clear a manner as I may, that this book would not be published were it not for the kind and generous hearts the Burgers. I had been at their kitchen table for no more than an hour, when Doug called about the book. Westbow Publishers had contacted him, but for it to be worthwhile to go forward, a considerable investment would have to be made. I no more had hung up the phone and that couple, whom I had just met, made a promise to pay that initial publishing costs for my memoirs. Their word has been just as true about financing the book as was Doug's in editing it. Thank you, Kathy and Jerry.

The writing took five years to complete (ed. note: five long years). During that time I served as interim pastor at Highland Park Presbyterian Church and Union Park Presbyterian Church in Des Moines. They both allowed me to use valuable study leave to get away to a secluded place where I could concentrate on the task at hand. I offer my deepest thanks to both of those churches for believing in my dream with me.

I do not have sufficient words to express my gratitude for the quiet and comfortable guest house that Dr. and Mrs. Bill Reed of Kansas City, Missouri, provided for me on two occasions for writing time. And I thank Rev. Don Fisher and his wife Laurie for making the request on my behalf to the Reeds. You will have read of my exploits with Don in Chapter III, and I say to his wife Laurie again, it was all Don's idea.

The first draft was completed, and then the question of importance was, "Who is going to read the manuscript and note all the grammar and punctuation mistakes?" It was embarrassing, to say the least, to ask anyone to assume that task. But in the end I have three people to thank for the intense reading required for that arduous undertaking. Joyce Rash, a retired English and Spanish teacher, corrected not only the English but also the Spanish phraseology in the book. Rev. Dawn Linder also did the read to correct errors in the manuscript, and make it ready for submission to the publisher. And I am grateful also to Rebecca Jones for the same task, as I know there were parts of the narrative that were very difficult for her to read. Thank you, Joyce, Dawn, and Rebecca.

Finally, I thank Aminu Abubakar, my friend from Ghana, who prayed incessantly during the writing of the book, that it be published and be a success.

Editor's Note

If the truth be known, this whole book thing was my idea all along. I recall reading Bob's journal of his time in El Salvador, as well as hearing stories about exploits whenever we happen to be in the same place, I knew then that it was a story that had to be heard by many. It is Bob's story, told from his heart, often broken by his experiences with the people of El Salvador. But it was my idea. So, what honor gets bestowed upon me for simply trying to be encouraging and upbeat about the idea? Well, here I am.

In truth, I am elated to have walked this journey with my dear and precious friend. It is his journey of faith, of redemption, of personal healing, and of trust in all that is Holy. Over the years, I have grown tired of seeing the faith that people claim to possess laid over their lives as a sort of window dressing. This is a story of one who knew different, someone who can dream dreams and sees visions, a person who can hear the call from the Eternal, and answer it with conviction. Bob is one of those rare people of faith who really has counted the cost, over and over, throughout the many years I have known him, and paid it. What's more, he also has the uncanny ability to get other well-intentioned, but unsuspecting, people to go along with him in his schemes, as you will read within. Those people, those congregations of the faithful, have done great work through sweat, generosity, and deep, deep faith. It is their story as well.

This is about Bob's journey with many special people, and many extraordinary people with him. I recall clearly a former colleague saying at a table in a hotel lounge to which we recessed following a presbytery meeting some years ago. Bob was there, but had just left the table, and the friend turned to me and said, *"You know, that guy really is a Christian, he takes this (bleep) to heart."*

Yes, it's true. My friend Cookie, as I have called him for years, is a Christian. But he is a devil of a writer, and I want everyone to know that this task has not been child's play. Bob is brilliant, and he has a prophet's heart. Bob has always had astonishing ways of expressing his thoughts, some of which even included punctuation. His opinions, memories, and insights expressed within capture our souls, but were not always easily discernable. Many times I pondered one sentence until my eyeballs turned to jelly. For the most part, I think the Spirit/Muse is pleased with what we have done in our collaboration and, it wouldn't have been so without the many precious lives that are written of within these pages, including Bob's own.

I am proud of my friend for reminding me of what it means to love God with one's whole heart, mind, soul, and strength, and to serve God's people with energy, intelligence, imagination, and love. And, I am damn proud to have played a small part in making these words available for many eyes and hearts to ponder.

And, please, don't bother calling me to point out what I overlooked or mistook.

> Doug Maben
> Knoll's Bed &Breakfast, North Platte, NE.
> July 1, 2011

CPSIA information can be obtained at www.ICGtesting.com
Printed in the USA
LVOW061754120312

272713LV00010B/21/P